I0020287

The Textual Warehouse

Bill Inmon

Ranjeet Srivastava

Technics Publications

2 Lindsley Road
Basking Ridge, NJ 07920 USA
https://www.TechnicsPub.com

Edited by Jamie Hoberman
Cover design by Lorena Molinari

All rights reserved. No part of this book may be reproduced or transmitted in any form or by any means, electronic or mechanical, including photocopying, recording or by any information storage and retrieval system, without written permission from the publisher, except for brief quotations in a review.

The authors and publisher have taken care in the preparation of this book, but make no expressed or implied warranty of any kind and assume no responsibility for errors or omissions. No liability is assumed for incidental or consequential damages in connection with or arising out of the use of the information or programs contained herein.

All trade and product names are trademarks, registered trademarks, or service marks of their respective companies and are the property of their respective holders and should be treated as such.

First Printing 2021
Copyright © 2021 by Bill Inmon and Ranjeet Srivastava

ISBN, print ed.   9781634629546
ISBN, Kindle ed. 9781634629553
ISBN, ePub ed.   9781634629560
ISBN, PDF ed.   9781634629577

Library of Congress Control Number: 2021940867

Acknowledgments

Special thanks to my two little angels and my wife for their continuous support while working on the book.

I am grateful to my mother and father, who have given me so much of themselves. Blessings of my parents are very important to me. I remember feeling an enormous sense of gratitude and appreciation for my late grandmother. I have a special place in my heart for her. This work is dedicated to my parents and to my grandmother.

I want to express my gratitude to two special people, Bill Inmon and Steve Hoberman. Bill is my inspiration behind this book. This masterpiece would not have been completed without Bill. Getting an opportunity to write with Bill is an honor. Steve was a tough reviewer. Indeed, in a positive sense though and detailed oriented one.

Thanks to all my well-wishers, family members, and friends.

Ranjeet

Contents

CHAPTER 1

About Text

Although about 90% of our business data is text, when it comes to business and business decision making, we often only use the 10% structured data—which is data captured in a format that can easily be understood or interpreted by the system.

This book focuses on data in a textual format. We will talk about the problem definition, core pain areas, and possible solutions for different use cases. We will also talk about the methodology to implement these solutions. We will talk about best practices. We will talk about the proven framework and technology that can help you create your own "textual warehouse" for the benefit of the business.

Text and Documents in the Corporation

Once there was an insurance company that did a lot of business. The insurance sold and serviced policies of all kinds. The insurance company had been in business for many years.

Business was good, and the insurance company processed many insurance policies in a day. Over time there were a lot of insurance policies that belonged to the insurance company.

The policies that were sold were essentially a lot of boilerplate. A boilerplate is a standard contract a lawyer draws up to generically apply to a line of business. There were auto boilerplate policies. There were liability boilerplate policies. There were home insurance boilerplate policies. There were life insurance boilerplate projects. There were a lot of policies and a lot of different policy types.

Each new customer selected from the available options. And occasionally, the salesperson had to write in specialized terms for a policy. This slightly changed the boilerplate contracts.

The boilerplate contracts were very similar to each other. The only real difference between boilerplate contracts was the particulars about the customer.

Back Office Processing

The typical boilerplate text has two types of information – identifying and qualifying text, and simple text.

The back office people process the policies after the policies have been written. The typical boilerplate insurance policy had two types of information – identifying and qualifying text, and simple text. The simple text described many of the terms and conditions applicable to the policy. The identifying text were the particulars that made the policy unique. The identifying text contained such things as policyholder name, address, and telephone number.

Qualifying text contains the policy qualification terms that talks about your duties and responsibilities to qualify for coverage. It contains qualifying events like, in case of health insurance - 'getting married' (i.e. once married during the policy period, the spouse will automatically be covered after formal intimation to the insurance company), 'having babies' (i.e. up to two kids can be covered into the policy), 'premium paid' (i.e. insurance policy will be null and void if premium not paid with 60 days of the due date), and 'in case of illness/disability/death' (i.e. party should inform the insurance company within six months of the incident to claim the policy amount).

Similarly in case of auto insurance, a qualifying text includes 'Accidental qualifications', 'Road side assistance', and 'Out of City hotel accommodation reimbursements'.

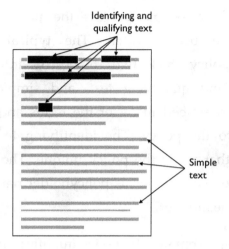

Fig 1.1 There are two types of text found in the policy.

Identifying and Qualifying Text

The identifying and qualifying text includes all of the information required to establish the unique identity of the policyholder, such as:

- Name
- Address
- Telephone
- Social security number
- Date of birth
- Policy identification number
- Policy coverage
- Agreed upon price
- Date of coverage

Simple Text

The simple text was the "fine print" of the boilerplate policy. Most of the simple text was written by a lawyer and specified terms and conditions, force majeure, cancellation language, enforcement date, and so forth. The identifying and qualifying text were the non-boilerplate fields found in the policy that the agent filled out upon the completion of the sale of the policy.

The Operational Database

Upon completion of the sale of a policy, the identifying and qualifying information from the policy was placed in a database, along with a lot of other information from other policies. Typically, the database was described as an "operational" database. The operational database was used in the insurance company's daily activity, such as for billing, premium payments, and claims management.

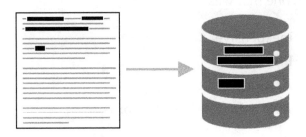

Fig 1.2 The identifying and qualifying data transfer to an operational database.

In the early days of the company, the documents were then filed in a cabinet. As long as there weren't too many documents, a cabinet sufficed.

One of the problems of filing insurance policies in a cabinet is that the policies could only be stored in a single order, usually by the name of the owner of the policy. If it were desired to search the filing cabinet documents in anything other than the order in which they were stored, making such a search was difficult.

Another problem with storing the policies in a cabinet was that – over time – the paper the document was written on began to deteriorate. In addition, If you misfiled a document in cabinets, it may never be found again. In order to find a lost document, it was necessary to go through all of the documents stored into the cabinet manually.

One day there simply were too many of the documents to be filed in a cabinet. A more permanent solution was needed, one that was:

- Inexpensive
- Efficient
- Accurate
- Able to handle lots of records

OCR (Optical Character Recognition)

At this point, the corporation brought in OCR technology. OCR technology was technology that allowed the document to be photographed. Once the document was photographed, it could be stored and managed electronically.

> *Optical character recognition, sometimes also called optical character reader or OCR, is the electronic conversion of typed, handwritten, or printed text into machine-encoded text, whether from a scanned document, a photo of a document or from subtitles. OCR can be used on various occasions for textual warehousing purpose.*

The text documents were sent to OCR – optical character recognition – for further processing. When processed by OCR the document was photographed. If there ever was a need to reference the document, the OCR image could be recalled. It was much more efficient and much less expensive to create and store the OCR image than storing the actual document itself.

OCR

Fig 1.3 The remaining text is sent to OCR.

Over time the number of records that went to OCR continued to grow. At first, there weren't too many. But over time, the volumes of OCR records grew.

Fig 1.4 The process of moving certain text to a database and other text to OCR is repeated over and over

Time passed, and the number of OCR documents grew and grew and grew. Soon there were a whole lot of OCR records.

The accumulation of the OCR records was not a problem when it came to storage. Storage was relatively inexpensive. And as long as the search for an OCR record was along the lines of the identifiable information (the identifying information and/or the qualifying information), the OCR records were not too difficult to work with.

But if it came to looking at OCR records on something other than identifying information, then there was a problem. On occasion, there was a need to look into the simple text. There are actually a lot of reasons why simple text from a long time ago needs to be examined:

- The simple text itself changes over time.

- The laws and regulations governing insurance change over time and affect the simple text.

- Business conditions change over time.

- The insurance company acquires other insurance companies creating the need to integrate records from both companies.

For many reasons, then, it may be necessary to go back and examine what the simple code says. When this is the case, finding information in the OCR record files is a difficult thing to do.

OCR Records Over Time

The first time there was a need to go back through the old OCR files, there was not much of a problem. At that time, there weren't too many OCR files. But over time, it began to be increasingly difficult to find anything. The more OCR files there were, the more difficult it became to rummage through them.

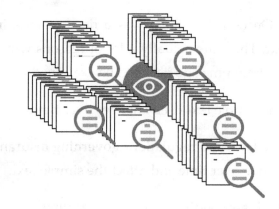

Fig 1.5 The information that was needed was hiding.

It became apparent that the simple information hiding in the OCR files was becoming lost.

The problem was that, in some cases, this simple textual information was needed as a vital component to day-to-day business operations.

Data in a Prison

It was recognized around this time that OCR records were effectively in prison.

The problem that has been described is not unique to the insurance industry. The problem of accumulating data covering and hiding behind older data that has been described is found – in one form or another – in practically every industry. The only difference between industries is how large the problem is and how fast the problem grows.

Another consideration is that the problem of finding text that is buried is hardly limited to insurance policies. Instead, the problem occurs for all sorts of documents, such as:

- Contracts
- Employment applications
- Warranties
- Home loan applications
- Email

Making the problem more challenging is that text does not fit comfortably well inside a database. Text is erose. It is remarkably inconsistent and databases require that its data be uniform and consistent. For these reasons and more, text presents a challenge to the analyst needing to manage it.

Information Buried Over Time

You can think of the problem of losing text like the problem of doing archaeology.

One day – thousands of years ago – a young Greek maiden was carrying an urn. For whatever reason, she laid the urn down beside a small bush. Then she walked away.

After a few years, the urn was covered with dust. After a few decades, the urn was covered with dirt. After a few millennia, the urn was covered with dirt up to six feet.

To find the urn, archaeologists had to uncover the centuries of earth that had covered the urn.

Year over year data volume mounts up to the point that nothing is able to be found except the most recent ones.

As time passes, there is this natural tendency to stack data upon data. After some time, the volume of data stacked mounts up to the point that nothing can be found except for the most current files.

CHAPTER 2

Document Anatomy

Documents, in their many forms, appear throughout the corporation and form the lifeblood of business. Documents provide the evidence for business transactions and memorialize business processes such as sales, marketing, and contracts. Documents track the life flow of business.

For example, an organized health insurance sector has primarily three core entities: Beneficiaries, Providers, and Payers. Beneficiaries can be me and you (the insured or the patients) who avail the facility of the provider. Providers can be a hospital or clinic, they can be government or private. Payers can be a health insurance company or the Government/Health Ministry who settles the claim(s) against the services extended by a provider to the beneficiary/insured.

Now let us talk about how "documents form the lifeblood of business and documents provide the evidence for business transactions." The healthcare beneficiary approaches the health insurance company to get insured. The insurance company prepares the "Insurance Policy Agreement" document between the insured and the insurance company. They (insurers) calculate the premium based on various "input parameters" provided by the beneficiary. Then the insurance company collects the premium from the beneficiary and issues a "Premium Certificate." After these business transactions, the beneficiary becomes 'insured'.

Now the insurance company collaborates with providers (hospitals and clinics). The insurance company gets into the "payer-provider agreement" with the providers to facilitate its services to their insured customers. They mutually get into "agreement" on extended "services agreement," "rates agreement," "discounts agreement," "claim process," "SLAs," "claim settlement agreement," and "claim rejection creteria."

Once an insured visits a provider/facility and avails the services fo the healthcare facility, the healthcare provider submits a claim to the payer and the payer honors the claims based on all those above agreements with the insured as well as with the provider.

Hence all the above-mentioned documents listed in double quotes are vital for the business and become the 'lifeblood of the business'. All those agreements, claims, claim settlements, claim rejection, and related documents become the 'evidence of the business transactions' for the health insurance business.

One Way to Look at a Document

There are many ways to classify and look at a document. Recall the way in Chapter 1 where a document contains two types of information, as shown in Fig 2.1.

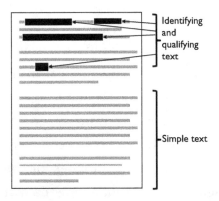

Fig 2.1 There are two types of text found in a document.

Identifying and Qualifying Information

Recall that when a document is finalized or memorialized, the identifying and qualifying information goes to a database for further analysis and processing. This identifying and qualifying information becomes the basis for doing what is known as transaction processing. In turn, transaction processing is a form of operational processing.

Identifying and qualifying text makes a document unique, and they will be different for each document. In car insurance, for example, name, phone number, address, car make, car registration number, year of manufacture, and so on, **identify** the document that the car insurance belongs to your specific car. And the insurance **qualifies** that you have roadside assistance, accessories coverage, passenger insurance, hospitalization expenses coverage, and so on.

The identifying and qualifying data goes into the database as transaction data that is operational in nature. You are paying your car insurance premium against your policy number or car registration number. If your car breaks down, you will call the insurance company and provide your car insurance policy number or car registration number. Based on your qualifying data, the insurance company will verify your claim and start the transaction by raising the request to extend their service of roadside assistance only while your policy is qualified the roadside assistance. If there is accessory damage in the accident, the claim will be accepted only if your insurance has accessory coverage. So based on your qualifying data, the claim will be initiated by your car service center, and if the claim is accepted by the insurance company, it will be settled by the insurance company to the service provider. This shows how identifying and qualifying information becomes the basis for doing transaction processing for the associated business.

The identifying and qualifying data goes to a database, which is typically a relational database. This database is typically called an "operational" database. The operational database is used for many purposes, such as:

- Billing
- Inventory control
- Accounts payable
- Customer analysis

Operational processing is the day-to-day activity of the corporation.

Storing the Documents

After the identifying information and the qualifying information is stripped off a document, the document is sent to storage. It is much more efficient and cost-effective to store large numbers of documents electronically than it is to store them physically. In addition, the longevity of the document is greatly extended by placing them on OCR, as paper deteriorates rapidly.

OCR

Fig 2.2 The remaining text is sent to OCR.

Different Document Types

Although there is a standard process for handling documents, many types of documents have many different sets of characteristics.

There is a large range of document types, each with its own set of characteristics—there is no such thing as a standard document.

There are many ways to classify a document. Some documents, including contracts, contain boilerplate. In the case of boilerplate, a lawyer writes a standard contract, and that contract is used repeatedly. The only thing that changes in boilerplate are contact details and perhaps a few terms based on the nature of the document or based on the document type or purpose.

Another type of document is a document where the content is almost never the same – unlike boilerplate. A typical document of this sort is a medical record. Each time there is a medical procedure or activity (an episode of care), the activity is recorded. The medical record tracks the individual activities of a patient through the medical process. It is very rare for a patient to have identical experiences as another patient.

Another type of document is a warranty claim. A warranty claim is created when a product that has been warrantied has had a problem. Each warranty claim is unique. However, because most warranty claims are small and because the circumstances behind the generation of the warranty claim tend to be similar, warranty claims are much more generic than medical records.

Another type of document is a legal deposition. A legal deposition is a document that is a recording of a conversation between a lawyer and someone who is involved in a lawsuit taken under oath. No two depositions are exactly the same.

There is then a wide difference between different document types.

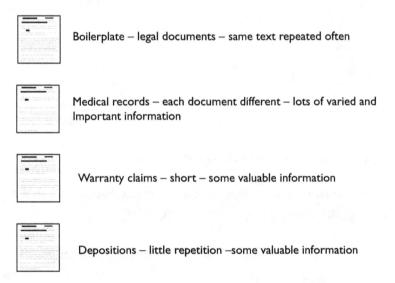

Boilerplate – legal documents – same text repeated often

Medical records – each document different – lots of varied and Important information

Warranty claims – short – some valuable information

Depositions – little repetition –some valuable information

Fig 2.3 Different types of documents.

Classifying Documents

There are variations across document types. The repeatability of the text is only one measure of the differences between document types. Repeatability means that the same content appears in all documents of similar types, such as a privacy clause or warranty information. Repeatability generally refers to boilerplate text content.

	LENGTH	REPETITION	SENTIMENT	RETENTION
Contracts	Long/ Medium	Yes	No	Long Term
Medical Records	Long/ Medium	No	No	Medium Term
Warranty Claims	Short	No	Yes	Medium Term
Depositions	Long	No	Yes	Short Term
Bill of Materials	Long/ Medium	To some extent	No	Medium Term

Fig 2.4 Document types and classification criteria.

Some of the other ways that document types can differ from each other include:

- Document length – some documents are long, some are short

- Repetition– there is a high degree or a low degree of repetition among documents

- Retention – some documents are kept for a long time while other documents are kept for a short time

- Sentiment – some documents express sentiment while other documents do not express sentiment

Challenges of Simple Text

Despite the differences between document types, some common obstacles exist in finding out what is in the simple text. To do simple text analysis, you have to overcome ALL of these challenges.

When it comes to simple text, we notice that only its name is 'simple' but its analysis is not simple. There are few obstacles that lead to make it complex. Like:

- Volume
- Quality
- Repetition
- Format variation
- Spreadsheet
- Document type
- Synonymous words

Obstacles to Analyzing Simple Text

When there is a large volume of text, the text that is useful and relevant "hides" behind all the text that is not useful or relevant.

The most common challenge to finding out what is in simple text stored in OCR is dealing with the volume of records. Depending on the document type, it is not uncommon to search many records to do text analytics on simple text. In addition to large volumes of text, it is common for the text that is useful and relevant to "hide" behind all of the other text that is not useful or relevant. The sheer number of records presents the first and largest obstacle in searching simple text.

Quality of Transcription

OCR doesn't perform well when unusual font, weak ink strikes, and/or aged/deteriorated quality of papers is used. Hence in any case OCR jobs need cautions scrutiny.

A second major obstacle to finding information in simple text stored in OCR is the transcription quality. In most circumstances, OCR does a good job of finding electronic text in the documents. But in some cases, OCR does not do a good job of transforming the snapshot image to electronic text. OCR can do a bad job if:

- The font used in the text is an unusual one
- The ink strike is weak
- The paper starts to deteriorate (may be due to aging or unusual storage or even due to the poor quality of the paper)

Any of these reasons will negatively affect the outcome of the quality of transcription doing an OCR job. Unfortunately, if the OCR transcription is not done well, there is little to nothing the analyst can do when it comes to analysis.

The OCR job needs to be validated cautiously. Obviously, if it is a small bunch of files/records, you can do it for every job. But when you have many records, analysis of each record is neither feasible nor logical. But yes, we can do a cautions sampling that is logically distributed among your different classification(s)/segment(s) of records.

```
1no".meo(ai Lo,rot Maini.n."~ ticen.ttd Lwacity
C~'Cffy...."u.tr'nen'-,5rbo....,
th. L,,,,,noed Cap""'!!, 6rJ012010 71112011. 111/20'
Pe'P*tuat M"\JI!II 6130120' , 6130120' 2 6130120' 3
1I(:..~• .o Perp4fUIW Support Eta...11f1. S.....o. a•
U,)It of Oventrty UnrlCo.1 UnltCc)'t·1 Cao-.clty Cap
Pfot.fuC11 MI.,ur.men( Unit Count .1'" USD!. \,nUSD)
```

Fig 2.5 Sometimes the quality of the OCR transformation is unusable.

We may consider different verification strategies like random sampling, automated verification, and related word matching to avoid any ambiguous business decision-making due to the wrong OCR output.

Highly Repetitive Text

On occasion, the simple text for a document type can be highly repetitive. The challenge presented by this occurrence is that there is wasted space if the repetition remains in the document. The same text may be stored exactly the same way millions of times. This does no one any good. In some cases, the wasted space is considerable. The challenge is to make the text searchable without wasting space.

Fig 2.6 Sometimes the text can be highly repetitive.

Non-Repetitious Text

The reverse of highly repetitious simple text is simple text that has little or no repetition. While there is no wasting of space, in this case, the issue here is that the mapping of text to metadata may require a large amount of resources. Each different document will require its own unique mapping. Metadata includes the taxonomy and 'mapping of the text to the metadata' in this case means 'mapping of the text to taxonomy.' Taxonomies will be covered shortly.

Little repetition leads to more unique text sets. More unique means more variance. More variance means mapping to each of those unique texts. Examples of documents with little repetition include medical records, discharge summaries, social media posts, blogs, complaint letters, service requests, free text feedbacks, review comments, and free text opinions.

Multiple Formats

In the same vein, there may be only one document type. But that document type may have multiple formats. Each format type may require its own unique mapping. Examples include product catalogs (for different products within the same company), restaurant menus (different restaurants within the same city or same cuisine), and national registration documents (like Land Registration, Vehicle Registration, Marriage Registration, Police Complaint Registration, Voter ID Registration, and Child Birth Registration). Such use cases are very fit for national digitization initiatives or smart city projects.

Text on Spreadsheets

Text is sometimes in a spreadsheet format. To be analyzed, the text needs to be removed from the spreadsheet and placed into a format that is amenable to word processing. And sometimes, this reformatting can be a complex task.

Text in Hiding

But one of the biggest challenges is that important words and phrases hide among a jungle of words and phrases that are not important. In this case, the process of doing text analytics is like an Easter egg hunt. You need to cover a lot of ground efficiently. So, the effort should be to capture the important words from the pool. The important words are needed for business decision-making and often used with business analytics—feedback words on food or service in the hospitality industry, or diagnosis and treatment words from healthcare.

Words that are supposed to be captured from the business text for your business analytics to help critical business decisions. So, missing important words will not help you achieve the purpose. You may be left behind in the business text analytics if those are ignored or missed. Hence try not to miss many important words out of the pool/mass of other words and phrases.

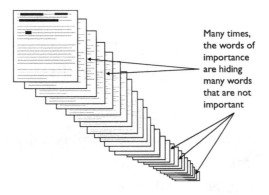

Many times, the words of importance are hiding many words that are not important

Fig 2.7 Important words and phrases can be hiding.

Multiple Document Types

Another obstacle to doing text analysis of simple text is that many different types of documents are mixed together. Mixing different document types makes the mapping process complex and arduous. Text analysis is most efficient if there are only a few types of documents that are mixed together. Here different types of documents mean documents with different business purposes.

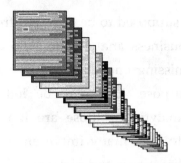

Fig 2.8 Different document types mixed together.

Different Words – Same Meaning

One of the most ubiquitous problems with analyzing simple text is the fact that, on many occasions, there is more than one rendition of the same word. One person says one thing, and another person says something else. The only issue is that they are both saying the same thing.

Suppose you were a policeman examining reports. One report has a man named Bill. Another report has a man named William. In another report, there is Willie. In another report, there is Billy. All of these names are different. But they all can refer to the same person. To do text analytics properly, there must be name resolution.

Another example, this one in the medical field, names like Lasix, Furosemide, Urex and Lodix are different names with the same meaning.

The Need for Context

Another ubiquitous problem is that of the recognition of context. You cannot do text analytics without recognizing both text and context. To do contextual analysis of text, you must go outside of the text to find the needed context. Text without context is meaningless. It can even be misleading. The term "context" may be said to consist of two components: the context and situational context (in linguistics, it is also called linguistic context and extra-linguistic context). Even context can be situational.

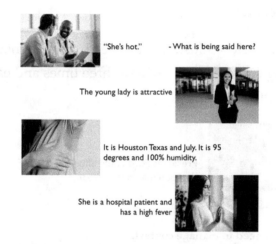

Figure 2.9 One day two men were talking.

Context refers to the text surrounding a message. This includes the textual elements that occur before and/or after a word, a phrase, or even a longer text or utterance. Why is it important? Because the context helps in understanding the particular or specific meaning of the word or phrase.

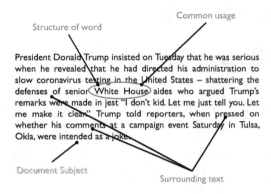

Fig 2.10 Recognizing context in simple text when doing analytics.

When you are disambiguating text, you must have both text and context.

The figure below illustrates the need for recognizing and managing context. 'Ford' is used three times and each time it has a different context.

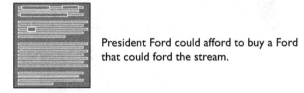

President Ford could afford to buy a Ford that could ford the stream.

Fig 2.11 The need to manage context.

Proximity Analysis

In some cases, the proximity of words plays a great role in their interpretation. Two words placed together have a different meaning than if the words are apart.

The Dallas Cowboys were once a great team…..

…………………………

The banks in Dallas would hardly make a loan to the poor, broken down cowboy and his pathetic horse.

Fig 2.12 The confusion of proximity.

Homographic Resolution

Yet, a more sophisticated text analytical conundrum occurs when the interpretation of a word depends on understanding who wrote the word. If the person writing "ha" was a heart doctor, then "ha" refers to heart attack. If the person writing "ha" was a general practitioner, then "ha" refers to headache. If the person writing "ha" was an endocrinologist, the person was referring to hepatitis A. To properly interpret "ha," you have to know who it was that write the term.

The patient had ha in the waiting room….

Ha – headache?
heart attack?
hepatitis A?

Fig 2.13 The need for homographic resolution.

There are then many challenges awaiting the person who must search for information from the simple text portion of a document.

These challenges are mitigated by the architectural feature called the textual warehouse.

Noun Search and Analysis

Consider restaurant or store feedback. A customer has written free text as their feedback, and they have written the name or rather a first name of the employee into the feedback sheet. The feedback can be positive or negative. Capturing such noun-based information and bringing them to a structured format is tricky. A reward for good feedback and a penalty for bad feedback might not go well if not handled accurately. A wrong outcome may lead to unwanted demotivating factors among direct beneficiaries. You may reward the one who had to be penalized and take corrective action against the employee who deserves a real reward.

For example, a few customers wrote feedback about 'Sanskriti Srivastava' being a great host. Some had written the feedback for 'Sanskriti Srivastava', some wrote only 'Sanskriti', some 'Srivastava', some may mistype the name to 'Shanskriti'. There are chances that the facility has more than one host with the last name 'Srivastava'. Noun handling is very important.

CHAPTER 3

Document Transformation

Working with simple text and documents inevitably involves the subject of OCR – optical character recognition. Often text has to pass through OCR before it passes through textual Extract, Transform, and Load (ETL) before loading into a textual warehouse. So, it is worthwhile taking a good and close look at text and OCR processing.

A Snapshot/Image

The explanation of OCR begins with what happens when OCR captures a document. The first step is that a snapshot (or image) of the document is taken.

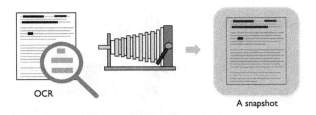

OCR

A snapshot

Fig 3.1 OCR is a simple image of a document.

In many ways, the snapshot is just what you get when you take a selfie. When all you have is an image, you cannot do any processing of the text that appears on the image.

Although the resulting snapshot is useful for legal document disclosure, it cannot yet be used for textual processing. You can see the text that is on the snapshot if you look, but you cannot use it for electronic text processing. One must convert the OCR image to electronic text to allow textual processing.

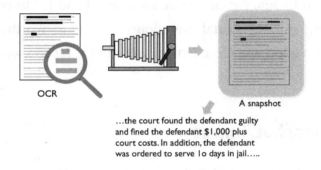

OCR

A snapshot

...the court found the defendant guilty
and fined the defendant $1,000 plus
court costs. In addition, the defendant
was ordered to serve 10 days in jail.....

Fig 3.2 Conversion of a document to electronic text.

Electronic Text

After taking the snapshot and producing the electronic text, the text can then be read and processed. However, sometimes there is a problem with the quality of lifting the electronic text off the snapshot. As long as the electronic text faithfully reproduces what is on the snapshot, there is no problem. But occasionally, the electronic text has errors. The snapshot may have a "j" that is interpreted as an "I." Or the electronic image may have a "/" where there should be an "1." When this misinterpretation occurs frequently, the text will not be usable, and there isn't a lot that can be done about it except to reprocess the document again.

Re-process doesn't guarantee the change in output. It can't be guaranteed that the next reprocess will fix the misinterpreted word. It depends on the OCR, whether it corrects the mistake(s) in the next iteration of the processing of the document.

There are few other ways of correcting such misrepresentation of words. But those might be very costly ways in case there are a large volume of documents.

The Quality of the Electronic Text

So what can you do to minimize the chances of text misinterpretation occurring?

Font

The first thing you can do is make sure that your OCR manufacturer can handle the font type. Some manufacturers handle different font types better than others. Despite common beliefs, there is no such thing as a standard font type. If the text has been printed with an unusual font type, the OCR may not react does well.

PIHU AND GUNGUN ARE SISTERS....

Pihu and Gungun are sisters....

Pihu and Gungun are sisters...

Pihu and Gungun are sisters....

Fig 3.3 The font type makes a big difference in whether OCR can accurately create electronic text.

The more "standard vanilla" your font type, the better the chances your OCR manufacturer can handle it. It also depends upon the OCR used. An OCR manufacturer might only support a few fonts, so we need to be selective in OCR selection. The more fonts supported, the better the OCR. Standard fonts like Verdana, Arial, and Times New Roman work with most of the OCRs.

Inkstrike

The second thing you should look for is inkstrike. Inkstrike is the degree that ink is transferred to paper during printing. Occasionally, when you get to the end of a printing ribbon, ink tank, or ink cartridge of the printer, the inkstrike becomes fainter and fainter. Or consider a little older scenario where occasionally the same printing ribbon was used so often that there was not much ink left on it. Or perhaps the printer was malfunctioning. For whatever reason, occasionally, the ink is printed so faintly that the OCR equipment cannot handle it well. The lighter the inkstrike, the more difficult it becomes for OCR to pick up the image.

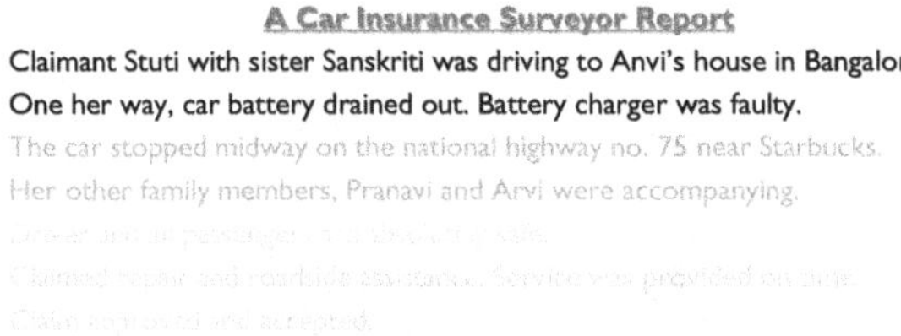

A Car Insurance Surveyor Report

Claimant Stuti with sister Sanskriti was driving to Anvi's house in Bangalore. One her way, car battery drained out. Battery charger was faulty. The car stopped midway on the national highway no. 75 near Starbucks. Her other family members, Pranavi and Arvi were accompanying.

Fig 3.4 Instrike makes a big difference in quality.

Paper Age and Fragility

A third factor that sometimes comes into play is the age and quality of the paper. Over time, paper becomes brittle and starts to deteriorate. If you are dealing with older paper, the age and fragility of the paper may become an issue when doing OCR processing.

OCR Manufacturer

A fourth factor in the quality obtained in doing OCR processing is the selection of the manufacturer of the OCR equipment. Some OCR processing is designed for occasional use, and other OCR processing is designed for heavy-duty, industrial-strength processing.

Handwriting

Be aware that OCR does not work well on handwriting. OCR technology works best on printed material.

Fig 3.5 OCR does not work on handwriting.

After the Fact Editing

You might be tempted to say that even if OCR does not read and interpret text properly that, after the fact, you can read and edit what OCR technology has produced and make corrections. This is not a good idea.

At best, based on our experiences, you can make a 1% improvement on the quality produced by OCR. And 1% is in the best case in any standard size assignment or engagement.

Large volumes of text arrive at the textual warehouse, making manual scanning and correction tricky and tiresome work. Let's discuss 'Manual processing' next.

Manual Processing

Another approach is to use OCR technology for all the documents that will work well with OCR and then use manual reproduction and transcription for the documents that won't work well with OCR. This approach works well if there are only a handful of documents that have to be reproduced manually. If there is any significant amount of manual reproduction required, this approach is costly and time-consuming.

Identifying Documents

It is noteworthy that documents can be identified by the document id known to OCR, by the internal identifying data contained in the document, or by both means.

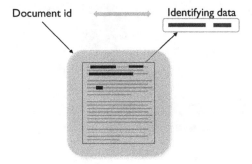

Fig 3.6 Any document can be identified.

If the document follows a standard template or format, we can have some document identification number for every document. If not, we will have to point to identifying data to help with uniquely identifying the document.

For example, a policy document can have a policy number as document id, but a feedback form can have a person's name and date/time as identifying data.

CHAPTER 4

Textual Warehouse Introduction

At the center of doing textual analytics and managing text in the corporation is an architectural feature known as the "textual warehouse."

Identifying and qualifying data from the document goes into a database. The important business-related text that does not go into the database goes into the textual warehouse.

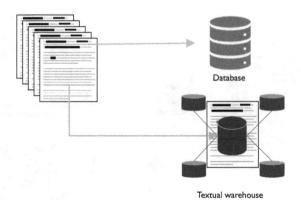

Database

Textual warehouse

Fig 4.1 The textual warehouse.

The textual warehouse contains the simple data that comes from documents. Fig 4.1 shows that the identifying and the qualifying data from the document goes into a database. The important business-related text that does not go into the database goes into the textual warehouse.

Where's the data warehouse?

To see the fuller picture, once the identifying and qualifying data is placed into a database, eventually that data finds its way into the data warehouse.

ETL is needed to make these transformations of data happen. Two forms of ETL are needed: standard ETL that integrates application data into a data warehouse and textual ETL, which transforms raw text into a textual warehouse.

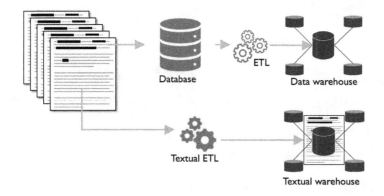

Fig 4.2 An architectural rendition.

Textual Warehouse – A Definition

A textual warehouse is a collection of business-relevant text that is referenced back to its source document. Usually, the text in the textual warehouse also contains the classification of the text.

As an example of what might be in a textual warehouse, there might be an entry that looks like:

- Red pony – word
- Farm animal – classification
- Book by John Steinbeck, NA128.68 – location
- 2087 (first byte) – byte address

The entry in the textual warehouse tells what the word that is being described is, what its classification is, where it can be found, and the byte address where it can be found in the source document.

Who needs a textual warehouse?

Who needs a textual warehouse? Anyone who:

- Has a large amount of text
- Has to store the text for a lengthy period of time
- Needs to periodically search textual documents

This list includes many organizations such as:

- Insurance companies
- Banks
- Finance organizations
- Government
- Manufacturers

Document types to store in a textual warehouse include:

- Insurance policies
- Contracts
- Bill of materials specifications
- Deeds of trust
- Warranties
- Medical records
- Patient discharge summary
- Human resource profile
- Automotive quality reports

When do you need a textual warehouse?

This answer is a little bit different for every company. There is no standard answer here.

For small organizations and startups, they can probably do without a textual warehouse. But at some point, in time, the volume of information to be managed starts to become overwhelming. When an organization reaches the point where they need textual documents to run their business properly and cannot find those documents easily and efficiently, they need a textual warehouse.

It is normal for an organization to experience challenges in managing its textual documents before building a textual warehouse. It is unusual for an organization to be proactive in the building of a textual warehouse. In fact, nearly all organizations build their textual warehouse in a reactive mode, where the pain level has risen to a critical point. Fig 4.3 shows that a certain period of time passes before an organization builds its textual warehouse.

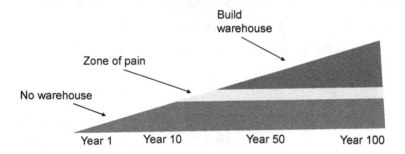

Fig 4.3 When a textual warehouse is needed.

So as shown in the image above, it doesn't mean that you need a textual warehouse only after 20-25 years of your business. The diagram above is symbolic only. The faster you generate text, the sooner you will need a textual warehouse.

Why do you build a textual warehouse?

There are two primary reasons why an organization builds a textual warehouse:

- As an aid to finding relevant documents, and
- As a basis for analytical processing.

Either or both of the reasons for building a textual warehouse can be found in an organization.

The second reason is obvious and the ultimate purpose. The first reason is related to cross-referencing the source of the data/text captured into the textual warehouse. So, the source document reference might be needed for various obvious reasons like Contracts, Agreements, Court Hearings, and Medical Transcriptions.

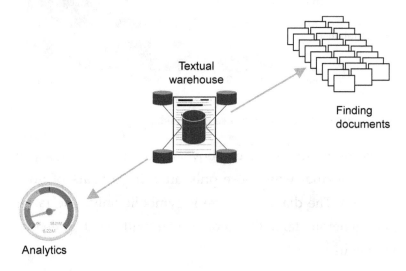

Textual warehouse

Finding documents

Analytics

Fig 4.4 The primary purposes of a textual warehouse.

Big Data

But for some organizations, there is another motive for building a textual warehouse. That reason is that infrastructure helps to find anything in Big Data. A lot of organizations invested in Big Data to understand the infrastructure that was needed. But for the most part, Big data never delivered on this part of the infrastructure. In this regard, a textual warehouse is a part of the infrastructure that can be used to help the end-user make the Big Data environment more effective. A textual warehouse can be useful for finding things in Big Data and even data lakes or data lakehouses, for various business-related textual analytics purposes.

Ingredients of Construction

There are two ingredients that are needed to design a textual warehouse. Those ingredients are:

- The raw documents of the organizations, and
- An understanding of the business itself.

The words and phrases that are important to the business form the basis for the design of the textual warehouse. To the database designer that does classical database design, it seems odd that there is no mention or even a reference to processes in the design of the text warehouse. Indeed, the textual warehouse design is very different from classical database design.

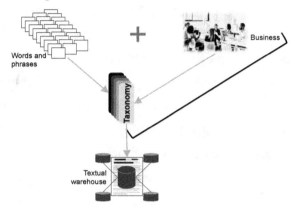

Fig 4.5 Very different from classical data base design.

The Operation of a Textual Warehouse

So how does the text warehouse environment operate? The operation of the text warehouse environment starts with the creation of the taxonomy.

The taxonomy is a list of the words and classifications of the business that are important to the business.

It is a classification of something. For example, we can classify car insurance, home insurance, life insurance, business insurance, bike insurance, and home appliances insurance as General Insurance. So General Insurance is the taxonomy of all those insurances listed above:

General Insurance

- car insurance
- home insurance
- life insurance
- business insurance
- bike insurance
- home appliance insurance

Once the taxonomy is created, the raw text is passed through textual ETL and the taxonomies help us find the important text. After the raw text is processed, the textual warehouse is created.

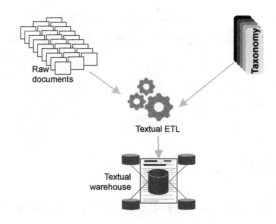

Fig 4.6 Constructing the textual warehouse.

The Output of a Textual Warehouse

What does the contents of the textual warehouse look like? The textual warehouse contains the collection of all the important textual words and phrases that are found in the raw documents.

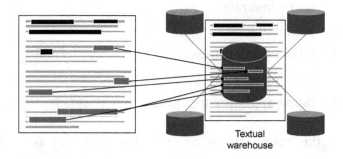

Fig 4.7 The transition from raw text to the textual warehouse.

Each entry in the textual warehouse consists of:

- The word or phrase that has been found
- The classifications of the words or phrases
- An identification of the source document
- The byte address of the word or phrase

Boilerplate Text

The one exception to the contents of the textual warehouse is boilerplate text. Boilerplate text appears over and over in each document. Contracts have a lot of boilerplate text. It is a waste of processing and space to repeat the same document analysis for each document.

A much more efficient way to handle boilerplate text is to process one document and save the results. The results then become the 'reference" document. Then when encountering other boilerplate documents, a simple reference to the reference document is made. Doing so saves much unnecessary processing and space. Fig 4.8 shows this economy of processing and space.

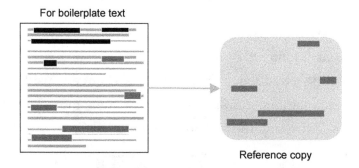

Fig 4.8 Make one reference copy of the boilerplate text.

For boilerplate text, simply store the reference information. This saves a huge amount of space and processing.

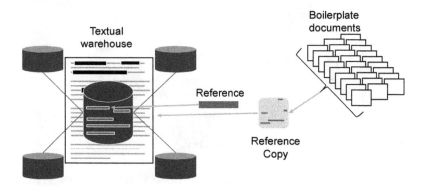

Fig 4.9 Store just the reference information for boilerplate text.

Changing the Taxonomy

The creation of the textual warehouse is a straightforward activity. But there is one factor that we need to consider. That factor is that the textual warehouse is never any more current than the taxonomy that was used in its creation.

Suppose that a textual warehouse is created at moment A. Then at moment B the taxonomy is changed. Either something is added or something is changed inside the taxonomy at moment B. Now suppose some more raw text is passed through the taxonomy at moment C.

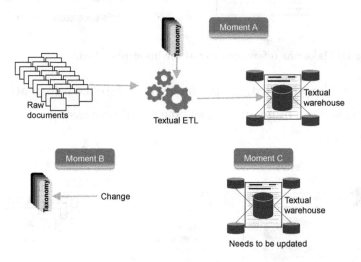

Fig 4.9 Making changes to the taxonomy.

The data inside the textual warehouse is now out of sync. The text inside the textual warehouse at moment A will be out of step with the text that was processed at moment C. The text processed after moment C will contain references not found in the text processed after moment A. Sometimes this difference in what has been captured and entered into the textual warehouse makes little or no difference. But sometimes this difference can be significant.

It is important to be sensitive and observant about any changes into the taxonomy that may lead to a difference in references and its direct impact on the textual warehouse.

CHAPTER 5

Taxonomies

The "brains" of building the textual warehouse is something called a taxonomy. The taxonomy directs all the activities and affects all of the outcomes made in building the textual warehouse. The simplest explanation of a taxonomy is that it is a classification of words. However, there is much more to a taxonomy than the simple definition would imply. The impact on the processed text is not obvious when first looking at the taxonomy.

A Simple Taxonomy

There are many taxonomies and many types of taxonomies. Here is an example of a simple taxonomy:

Car
Audi
Porsche
Ford
Suzuki
Tata
Mahindra
Ferrari
Honda

Fig 5.1 A simple taxonomy.

Fig 5.1 shows that there can be many different makes of cars. There can be Audis, Porsches, Ford, and Chevrolet. Note that only makes of cars are found in this list. There are no horses, motorcycles, roller skates, or airplanes found in this list. If something other than a make of car were in the list, it would not be a taxonomy because it might not be part of the same classification of like words. Each of those things are a different classification of a make of car. Only makes of cars are found in this taxonomical classification. If you wanted to have a different taxonomy that would include engine parts, such as cam shaft, carburetor, and piston, you could certainly create such a taxonomy. But it would be a different taxonomy than the taxonomy of automobile make.

Of course, there are many, many different kinds of taxonomies. (In fact, there are probably an infinite number of different classification types.) Some of the other classification types look like these:

Car	Tree	Animal	Country	Domicile
Audi	Elm	Tiger	India	House
Porsche	Pecan	Bear	USA	Apartment
Ford	Oak	Rabbit	England	Condominium
Suzuki	Sequoia	Lizard	Germany	Cave
Tata	Mesquite	Skunk	Japan	Boat
Mahindra	Mango	Racoon	Australia	
Ferrari		Coyote		
Honda				

Fig 5.2 There are many types of taxonomies.

In Fig 5.2 it is seen that there are taxonomies for cars, trees, animals, countries, and domiciles. And in truth, there are taxonomies for insects, birds, diseases, religions, materials, guns, hats, and walking canes. There are as many taxonomies as there are ways to think of something. When doing text analytics, the challenge is to choose the right taxonomy for analysis.

There is a relation between raw text and taxonomy. We create a taxonomy using raw text as well many a time.

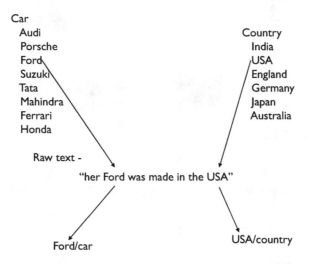

Fig 5.3 How raw text relates to a taxonomy.

Taxonomies and Data Models

In many ways, the taxonomy is to text analytics and the textual warehouse, as the data model is to the database designer and database design. The taxonomy plays the role of supplying the intellectual roadmap of how text is organized and relates together. The taxonomy is the "brains" of text analytics and plays the role of organizing the textual warehouse.

Fig 5.4 shows the equivalency of taxonomy to textual warehouse played by data model to database design.

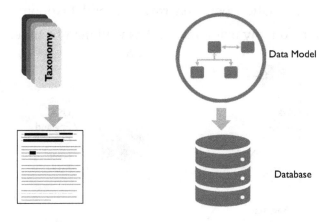

Fig 5.4 A taxonomy is to text what a data model is to a database.

Ontologies

An ontology is a group of related taxonomies.

In Fig 5.5, it is seen that there are three taxonomies – one for country, one for state, and one for city. The state taxonomy relates to the country taxonomy. In this case, the state of New Mexico is related to the country USA. And the city of Santa Fe is found in the state of New Mexico. Together the three related taxonomies form an ontology.

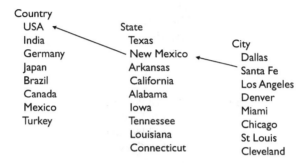

Fig 5.5 An ontology is made up of related taxonomies.

The Value of a Taxonomy

There is great value in creating and applying taxonomies to text. One of the values is in the savings a taxonomy makes when it comes time to analyze text.

In Fig 5.6 it is seen that an analyst wants to search text. The analyst wants to look for cars. Without a taxonomy to rely on, the analyst has to make an individual search for each type of car. The analyst looks for a Porsche. Then the analyst looks for a Ford. Then the analyst looks for a Honda. The number of searches the analyst has to do is for every type of car that there is. In addition, the analyst may forget to look for a car type. Suppose there is a Holden in the text. The analyst forgets to do a search for a Holden.

Car
  Audi
  Porsche
  Ford
  Suzuki
  Tata
  Mahindra
  Ferrari
  Honda

Search and find all Porsches
Search and find all Fords
Search and find all Hondas
Search and find all Chevrolets
....

or

Search and find all cars

Fig 5.6 Taxonomies simplify and streamline analytical processing.

However, when the analyst has a taxonomy available from a reliable source, the analyst merely states that the search is for a car. Because of the taxonomy, the system recognizes the many types of car that there are, including Holdens. In this regard, taxonomies greatly simplify and streamline the analytical searches that have to be done.

Where do taxonomies come from?

One of the interesting questions is where do taxonomies come from? The answer is that there are actually many sources for a taxonomy.

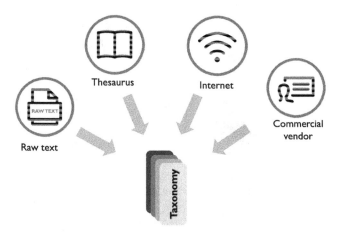

Fig 5.7 Where do taxonomies come from?

One source of taxonomies is the derivation of taxonomies from raw text. This can always be done. Another place taxonomy can be derived from is a robust thesaurus. The problem with a thesaurus is that it is easy to include words that don't belong in the taxonomy. A third source for a taxonomy is the Internet. Some taxonomies are public domain on the Internet. A fourth source of taxonomies is vendor-supplied taxonomies. There are vendors that have commercially available taxonomies for sale.

One advantage of acquiring a vendor-supplied taxonomy is that the vendor will supply updates to the taxonomy. Language is constantly changing. New words appear every day. The taxonomy needs to keep track of and be aware of the changes.

When you acquire a taxonomy from a vendor, usually the vendor supplies the periodic updates.

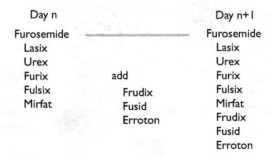

```
        Day n                              Day n+1
     Furosemide    ──────────────────   Furosemide
       Lasix                               Lasix
       Urex                                Urex
       Furix              add              Furix
       Fulsix            Frudix            Fulsix
       Mirfat            Fusid             Mirfat
                         Erroton           Frudix
                                           Fusid
                                           Erroton
```

Fig 5.8 Taxonomies change over time.

Word Resolution

Another of the many uses of a taxonomy in textual analytics is using a taxonomy to resolve aliases or alternate words for the same object.

For example, there may be medications that have different names. Different hospitals, pharma companies, and doctors have different names for the same object. For example, furosemide is also commonly known as Lasix. Or OJ Simpson is known as 'the juice."

```
   Furosemide              OJ Simpson
     Lasix                   O J Simpson
     Urex                    Orenthal James Simpson
     Furix                   the Juice
     Fulsix                  O. J. Simpson
     Mirfat                  OJ
```

Fig 5.9 One practical use of taxonomies is to directly connect unrelated words that mean the same thing.

Libraries of Taxonomies

It should come as no surprise that there are whole libraries of taxonomies. There are taxonomies for positive sentiment and negative sentiment. There are taxonomies for terms of negation. There are taxonomies for conjunctions and connectors. There are taxonomies for chemical engineering and aeronautical engineering. There are taxonomies for automobiles and horse buggies. There are, in fact, a lot of different kinds of taxonomies.

Taxonomies can be broken into different classes. There are generic taxonomies and there are specific taxonomies. A generic taxonomy is a classification of words that exist regardless of the subject. Positive sentiment is an example of a generic taxonomy. It doesn't matter what you are talking about when you say:

- I love ...
- I like ...
- I want ...

You could be talking about snails, hamburgers, or racing cars. It just doesn't matter what you are talking about when you use a generic taxonomy.

Specific taxonomies, on the other hand, are specific to some discipline or mode of thinking. For example, in an automobile manufacturing taxonomy, you would have a bill of material, a WIP specification, an inspection component, and so forth.

It is important to note that the taxonomies exist external to the text being analyzed. The taxonomies reflect classifications that exist even if no raw text exists.

The textual warehouse is created by passing raw text from the project through textual ETL. Textual ETL uses taxonomies to identify and classify the raw text and the textual warehouse.

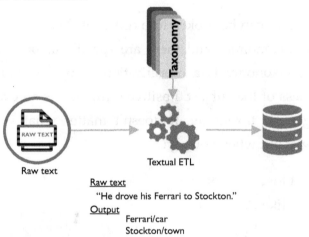

Fig 5.10 The mechanics of taxonomic resolution.

The output from the processing done by textual ETL is a pairing of the word found in the raw text and its classification from the taxonomy. In addition, the byte where the word was found is added to the textual warehouse and the identification of the source document is made.

CHAPTER 6

Textual ETL

The textual warehouse is created by running raw text into textual ETL. The operation of textual ETL is actually quite simple. The raw text is input. The other input is a series of appropriate taxonomies. There is other input as well. The output is the textual warehouse.

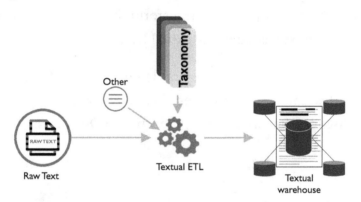

Fig 6.1 Running textual ETL.

Reading Raw Input

Textual ETL reads natively .docx, .doc, .txt, .html and .pdf to process text data and to help create the textual warehouse.

There are all sorts of raw textual input that can go into textual ETL. In a way, textual ETL is like a big vacuum cleaner that digests practically everything in its way.

The easiest form of raw textual input into textual ETL is electronic text. Electronic text appears in email and other computerized messages. Textual ETL can also ingest raw paper-based content. Raw paper is ingested by passing the paper and its contents through OCR. The electronic text option is turned on in OCR, and textual ETL reads the electronic text from OCR. The other source of raw textual input is from voice recordings. The voice recording goes through transcription to transform into electronic text, which is then passed on to textual ETL.

Textual ETL operates in several languages. The languages that textual ETL processes include English, Spanish, Portuguese, Italian, German, French, and Dutch.

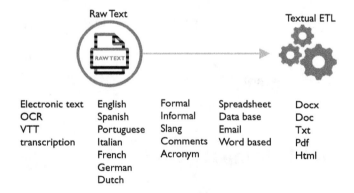

Electronic text	English	Formal	Spreadsheet	Docx
OCR	Spanish	Informal	Data base	Doc
VTT	Portuguese	Slang	Email	Txt
transcription	Italian	Comments	Word based	Pdf
	French	Acronym		Html
	German			
	Dutch			

Fig 6.2 The forms of raw input that textual ETL can operate on.

Textual ETL operates on formal text, informal text, comments, slang, and other forms of text.

Textual ETL can ingest raw text found on spreadsheets, databases, email, and other word-based sources. The text types that textual ETL reads natively includes .docx, .doc, .txt, .html and .pdf. There may be other forms of text that can be read and ingested by textual ETL.

Textual ETL and Transformations

Textual ETL does all sorts of transformations of text as the textual warehouse is being created. Most notably, textual ETL does taxonomic resolution. The appropriate taxonomy or taxonomies are selected for processing. They are then fed to textual ETL.

Textual ETL does lot more than taxonomic resolutions.

The raw text is read, and when a word for the taxonomy is found in the raw text, it is identified along with the classification of the word. In addition, the byte address of the word and the document id is stored as well. This information becomes the bedrock information found in the textual warehouse.

Raw text -

"the Beatles and Fleetwood Mac played at the Emporium…"

Output -

Beatles/rock group, byte 3091, c:/review0028
Fleetwood mac/rock group, byte 3103, c:/review0028
Emporium/event center, byte 3130, c:/review0028
…………………………..

Textual ETL

Fig 6.3 Taxonomic resolution.

But taxonomic resolution is not the only activity done by textual ETL. There are a wide variety of other tasks accomplished by textual ETL. Some of those tasks include:

- Stop word resolution
- Alternate spelling resolution
- Stemming
- Custom variable resolution
- Proximity resolution
- Homographic resolution

As an example of some of the kinds of transformations found in textual ETL, consider the raw text:

```
"John Jones, PS-19872, had the honour…"
```

In this case, custom variable processing determines that "PS-19872" is the designation for a patient. In addition, alternate spelling determines that "honour" can also be spelled "honor." And there are many other transformations that can be made of the raw text as it is turned into the textual warehouse.

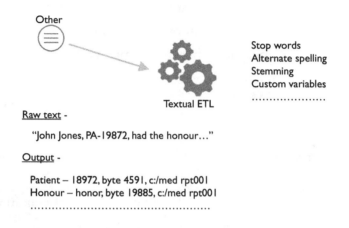

Fig 6.4 Other forms of transformation.

Textual ETL Output

The output from textual ETL can be put into any database format as it is database agnostic. Typical formats that you can put textual ETL output into include:

- Oracle
- SQL Server
- Teradata
- DB2
- Hadoop

Textual ETL has no special bias towards a relational database, although it certainly supports a relational database. But there is a good reason why relational databases are included. Relational databases support many different kinds of analytical packages. The richness of their support for analytical packages means that relational databases have to be supported.

An example

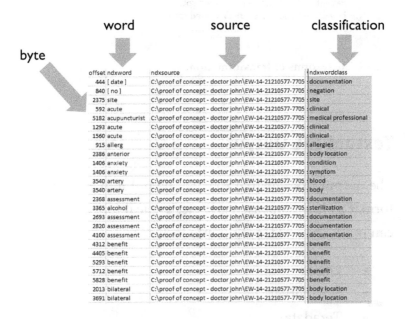

Fig 6.5 The contents of a text warehouse after textual ETL processing.

The data in Fig 6.5 comes from a series of medical records. In the database is found:

- The byte address of the word
- The word itself
- The document name – source name
- The classification of the word.

Once the textual warehouse has been created, all sorts of analysis can be done from the data that has been collected. You can do:

- Sentiment analysis
- Corelative analysis
- And project-specific analysis.

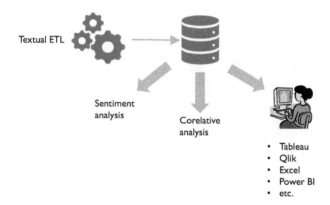

Textual ETL

Sentiment analysis

Corelative analysis

- Tableau
- Qlik
- Excel
- Power BI
- etc.

Fig 6.6 Once the Textual Warehouse is built, it can be used for all sorts of analysis.

CHAPTER 7

Textual Warehouse Design

The first step in building the textual warehouse is to find and create a taxonomy containing the needed words. In some cases, a taxonomy already exists and can be used as is. In other cases, a taxonomy has to be created from raw text. And yet, in other cases, an existing taxonomy exists but needs to be updated or customized.

The analyst determines which of these possibilities is the most relevant by looking at the text that needs to be captured in the textual warehouse and then determining if the organization can use an existing taxonomy. If there is not an existing taxonomy, then the organization must either create one or otherwise acquire one.

Business Definition

Another ingredient is the specification of the business definition that will be encompassed by the taxonomy. The business definition determines the scope of the taxonomy. If there is no business definition that is used as the starting point, then there will never be an end to the taxonomy.

The business definition can be either loosely defined or formally defined. In either case, the business definition must determine the boundaries of the taxonomy used in the creation of the textual warehouse.

Iterative Development

As with all of the steps in creating the textual warehouse, the building of the taxonomy is iterative. First one type of text is added. Then another type and modifications are made. The iterative process continues until the text encompasses all the major subjects that define the business definition.

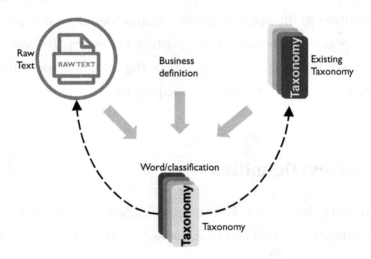

Fig 7.1 Step 1: Prepare the taxonomy.

Processing Raw Text

After preparing the taxonomy for the textual warehouse, the next step is to start processing raw text. Accomplish this step by using textual ETL (or textual disambiguation). The input to textual ETL is the prepared taxonomy and the raw text that needs to be processed. In addition, we can define other processing parameters.

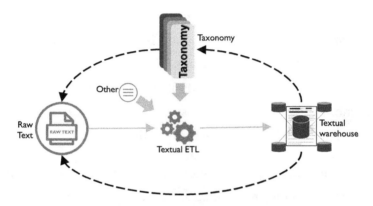

Fig 7.2 Step 2: Running textual ETL iteratively.

Iterative processing means we run a small sampling of the documents through, check the results, then go back and make necessary changes to textual ETL and/or the taxonomy. It is not good to run a significant amount of text through textual ETL in the first few passes. That is because it is highly likely that changes will have to be made and that the raw text will need to be rerun.

Therefore in running this step, a single small set of raw documents at a time makes sense.

The processed text can be put in a working area and saved for other text to be processed. The result is that text run through textual ETL is additive. The raw text does not have to be processed in a single large step.

Analytical Processing

The analyst role is very important in this whole textual disambiguation process lifecycle - from taxonomy validation to textual ETL transformation logic to business definition and business needs mapping and maturing the taxonomy for desired business outcomes. It helps make a robust business textual warehouse ultimately.

After the database is created, the database is ready for processing. Note that the entire database does not need to be created for analysis to occur. After the first few results are entered in the database, analysis can commence. Note that these early analyses are only partial results. But they still are useful for the analyst to start to work on.

Now analysis can occur. But the textual warehouse can start to be used to find data and documents in the corporation.

It is worth noting that the three steps outlined can certainly be intermixed when it comes to iterative corrections to the data.

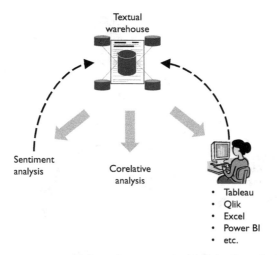

Fig 7.3 The analytical processing that occurs after the database has
   been created.

Inter Step Iterations

When the analyst is doing analytical processing, it is not
unreasonable to have to return to the building of the
taxonomy to make changes. Or the analyst may return to
the specifications found in textual ETL. Or the analyst may
go to the raw text. There is no limit to where the analyst
can go to adjust data and processing.

The ability of the analyst to make changes greatly
facilitates the job needed to be done by the analyst. Many
analysts have the attitude, "Give me what I say I want,
then I can tell you what I really want."

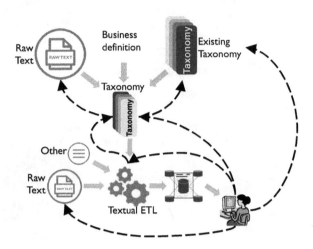

Fig 7.4 The intermixing of the major steps of development.

At first glance, it appears that the analyst does not know what they are doing. But that is not the case—the analyst operates in a mode of discovery. The analyst does not know what he/she wants until the analyst can see what the possibilities are. When the analyst changes his/her mind, the analyst is merely going through the discovery process.

Great Flexibility

The data found in the textual warehouse can help you build almost anything your business wants to see, from simple to complex.

In many ways, the data found in the textual warehouse is like Lego®. You can build almost anything with Lego blocks. You can build simple things. You can build complex things. You can build entire cities if you wish. The textual warehouse affords you the same possibilities. Your analysis can be as simple or as complex as you like. It is strictly up to you. Furthermore, given Lego's nature of the textual warehouse, you can change your mind whenever you like.

Requirements

A data warehouse has a data model, and a textual warehouse has a taxonomy.

The classical way to build systems is to start with requirements. And in this regard, analysis done in the textual warehouse environment is no different. But there is a major difference between classical development and analysis in the textual warehouse environment. A data warehouse has a data model, and a textual warehouse has a taxonomy. That is the first and most obvious difference.

But there are other differences. Another difference is that in the textual warehouse environment, the requirements are always changing. In the textual warehouse environment, requirements are fluid. The first iteration of analysis starts with a set of requirements. And the second iteration of analysis also has its own set of requirements.

But the requirements for the second iteration may be entirely different from the requirements for the first iteration of development in the textual warehouse environment.

Classic DW requirements are mostly static but textual warehouse requirements are always changing.

In the classical development environment, the requirements are essentially static. The requirements do not significantly change in the classical development environment. But in the text warehouse environment, the requirements are constantly changing.

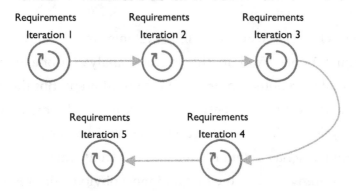

Fig 7.5 The fluid nature of the changing requirements in the textual warehouse environment.

A Balancing Act

In many ways, the development and analysis done in the textual warehouse are a balancing act. On the one hand, the analyst wishes to complete his/her analysis. On the other hand, the analyst constantly has to go back and make changes to the system. After those changes are made, the system needs to reprocess the data, because the data is now out of date after changes or updates in the system (including textual ETL) or taxonomy. The life of the analyst is one of constantly having to change modes of operation. And each of these modes must be accomplished in a balanced manner.

Development Differences

There is no doubt that the companion of the textual warehouse is the data warehouse. In many ways, these two complement each other. But when it comes to development, the data warehouse and the textual warehouse have some significant differences.

One difference is in terms of the treatment of requirements. In the data warehouse, as the data model is being built, if it is discovered that there is a problem or anomaly with the source data, the analyst can always go and modify the source data. But in the textual warehouse environment, if there is a problem, the analyst cannot go and make a correction. **It may even be illegal to go back and change text, even when the text may contain an anomaly.**

Think about the source of your textual warehouse—it can be your corporate contract, legal documents, agreement papers, signed letter of intent, and so forth. Do you think you can go back to the above listed source documents and do the changes you want to fix the problem or anomaly? No, it will be illegal. That is why we should note that in the classic data warehouse, we can fix the data anomaly in the source, but we can't fix the source in the textual warehouse.

Another difference is in terms of the usage of ETL. It is possible to build a data warehouse with homemade ETL. (It is not recommended, but it is possible.) But it is almost impossible to build a textual warehouse without textual ETL. For various reasons, build the textual warehouse with standard textual ETL. Trying to build your own version of textual ETL is not recommended. Stated differently, textual ETL is drastically more complex than classical ETL because textual ETL deals in various aspects of text handling including stop word resolution, alternate spelling resolution, stemming, custom variable resolution, proximity resolution, homographic resolution, and many more apart from taxonomic resolutions.

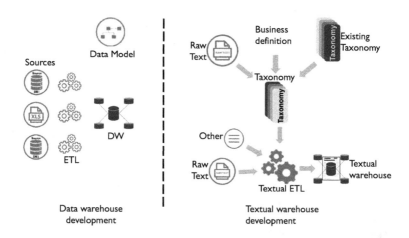

Fig 7.6 The different development environments.

CHAPTER 8

Design Elements

The design of the textual warehouse environment is somewhat different than the design of other databases and systems. In classical systems design, one of the major components is that of database design. But in the textual warehouse environment, there is no database design. In the textual warehouse environment, the databases are all fixed format databases. This means that the design work for a database in a textual warehouse is what goes into those fixed format databases, not the design of the database itself.

A Fixed Format Database

So, exactly what are the fields of data that are found in the fixed format found in the textual warehouse environment?

There are four basic fields of data in the textual warehouse fixed format database. Those fields are:

- Byte address – the byte address in the document of the analyzed word.

- Word – the word that has caught the attention of the analyst in reading the document.

- Document source – the identification of the source of the document.

- Classification – the taxonomical classification of the analyzed word.

Each of these fields of data have their own importance.

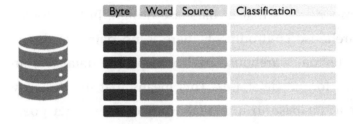

Fig 8.1 What the database looks like.

Byte address and document source is for tracking back the word and maintaining the exact correlation with the actual source of data/word. Word and classification is part of taxonomy and helps to classify the work taxonomically. The byte address is necessary for the resequencing of the words, in case sentiment analysis or other analysis is needed. When a word is placed in the database, it loses its position in the document if byte is not included. If there is ever a need to go back and to resequence the words in the order that they appear in the document, you must have the byte address.

The word being analyzed is important. It is selected from the document as the document is being read. The document identification is necessary because you can't find the document if you don't have its identifying specification.

The classification from the taxonomy is useful when analyzing the words that have been selected. In addition, classification is useful in other types of processing, such as sentiment analysis.

Inline Contextualization

There are many ways text can be selected from a document. One of those ways of selection is done by inline contextualization.

Inline contextualization is used when the text is predictable.

If text is not predictable, then you cannot use inline contextualization. Typical predictive text environments include corporate contracts, laboratory reports, and deeds.

Inline contextualization operates based on finding a beginning delimiter and an ending delimiter within the text itself. The delimiters can be specified because they are predictable in the text being analyzed. Anything lying between the two delimiters is selected for the database.

Beginning delimiter - Operative text - Ending delimiter

Beginning delimiter   Operative text   Ending delimiter

Managing director – Bill Inmon – declares that the statement......

Fig 8.2 An example of inline contextualization.

The beginning delimiter is "Managing director." The ending delimiter is "declares." The word or phrase that is selected is "Bill Inmon." The beginning delimiter and the ending delimiter will appear in every occurrence of the documents being analyzed.

Note that finding the ending delimiter can be complex on occasions. On occasion, it appears that there is no ending delimiter. Suppose you had an employment application where you had a field "Name:" and "Referrer Name:." A person would enter his/her name and the name of the person who referred him/her. It would appear that there was no delimiter at the end of both Name and Referrer Name. The text would look like:

- Name: Nawneet Kishore
- Referrer Name: Naveen Kumar

But there is a delimiter at the end of the line. It is just that the delimiter is hidden from sight. The delimiter is what is called a special character (such as an end-of-line character). In cases like this, the special character is in fact in the document, even though it is hidden.

Taxonomic Resolution

Taxonomies are used when the text is unpredictable.

Another common way to select text for inclusion into the database is by taxonomic resolution. A taxonomy is created external to the application. The taxonomy is used for comparison to the raw text by textual ETL. When a word in the raw text matches a word in the taxonomy, a database record is written.

Taxonomy
Car
  Porsche
  Ford
  Honda
  Toyota
  Ferrari
  Tata
  Mahindra
  ....

"...pulled her Porsche alongside the Toyota and commenced to engage..."

Porsche/car
Toyota/car

Fig 8.3 The usage of a taxonomy for selecting text to go into a textual warehouse database.

Taxonomies are used for unpredictable text, such as emails, conversations, and memos. Because unpredictable text is more common than predictable text, taxonomic resolution is much more common than inline contextualization.

Boilerplate Text

Recall boilerplate text occurs when a document is created and then the document is used repeatedly. A simple example of this is contracts. The lawyer creates a contract governing the sale of a product. Every time a new customer signs up, the same contract is used, over and over. The only thing that changes from contract to contract is the name of the person on the contract and items like, age, address, phone, and a few special clauses (if any).

Doc ABC	Doc BCD	Doc CDE	Doc DEF	Doc EFG
Reserved...	Reserved...	Reserved...	Reserved...	Reserved...
Signed	Signed	Signed	Signed	Signed
Dated...	Dated...	Date...	Date...	Date...
Officer...	Officer...	Officer...	Officer...	Officer...

Boilerplate – the same information repeated
many, many times

Fig 8.4 When boilerplate is placed in the textual warehouse environment.

In Fig 8.4 it is seen that the same text appears repeatedly in the textual warehouse. The problem with this is that it is wasteful of space. If it were only a few records, there would not be a problem. But when there are millions of records to be processed, unnecessarily repeating the same information is useless.

A Reference Document

There is another approach that achieves the same goals but does not waste huge amounts of space. That approach is to create a reference document. The reference document is built from the boilerplate text. Only one copy of the reference document is made. That document applies to all the records that will refer to it. The subsequent records that are created reference the reference document and do not reference individual words.

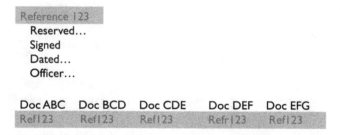

Fig 8.5 Each document refers to a reference number, saving huge amounts of space.

After building the reference document, the remaining documents are processed. When it comes time to create the data for the textual warehouse, the document merely refers to the reference document. In doing so, we save space and processing. If there are a lot of documents to be processed and if the reference document is large, there may be considerable savings.

Standard Contract Modifications

Now what happens when individualized modifications are made to the document? Suppose someone wants a change in terms. Or someone else wants special pricing. In this case, the reference document is modified on a case-by-case basis. The boilerplate has been modified.

It is easy enough to add individual specifications for the modifications that are required.

Reference 123
    Reserved...
    Signed
    Dated...
    Officer...

Doc ABC	Doc BCD	Doc CDE	Doc DEF	Doc EFG
Ref123	Ref123	Ref123	Refr123	Ref123
Add pricing		Add term		Add extension
				Add pricing

Fig 8.6 Each document refers to a reference number and addenda is added to the document where appropriate.

Probability of Access

One of the major and strategic decisions made about data found in the textual warehouse is deciding the best place to put data. It is normal for some textual data to have a very low probability of future access. This data belongs in archival storage. But other textual data found in the textual warehouse will have a higher probability of access. If the probability of access is high, then that textual data should be placed in active storage.

One of the issues here is the assessment of the probability of access. Who can look into the future and accurately predict what will happen someday far off? The answer is that no one really knows what is going to happen in the future. But you can make a reasonable guess as to what future activity and uses of certain data will be. And certainly, the business analyst, functional guy, SME, or stakeholder will be in a position to give you a clear picture of the probability aspects of the data.

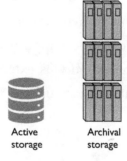

Active   Archival
storage   storage

Fig 8.7 The textual warehouse can use different forms of storage.

The Names Challenge

Inline contextualization is the best bet for capturing names.

One of the challenges of text analysis and the selection of words is that presented by names. Names are simple enough: John, Mary, Peter, and Allen. But names present a real challenge to the text analyst. The challenge comes in picking the name out of raw text.

Suppose we have the raw text of:

```
"The coach picked John up and threw him
                backwards."
```

How can we recognize that John is a person and is part of the description of what is transpiring? One way to do this is to have a taxonomy with all the commonly used names in the taxonomy. The taxonomy would be huge. Furthermore, the taxonomy would be eternally changing.

In addition, if the name taxonomy were to extend to countries outside the primary area of focus, the names found would be enormous. Suppose the taxonomy were created for the US and then was extended to India. India has many names that are unfamiliar to US citizens.

US First Names:	Indian First Names:
John	Shalini
Mary	Anamika
Bill	Pankhuri
Terry	Lalbabu
Sandra	Shobha
Joe	Ranjeet
…........	…........

Fig 8.8 India has many names that are unfamiliar to US citizens.

Another issue is that of last names. While there is a certain similarity of first names, there is no similarity of last names anywhere. First names are relatively uniform; last names are not uniform at all. Look at these Indian last names:

- Srivastava, Shriwastav, Shriwastaw, Shriwastva, and Sriwastaw reused interchangeably for the same or similar last name. Sometimes by mistake/mistyping or unknowingly.

- Verma and Varma are sometimes used interchangeably.

And the name can be any name, not only the name of a person. It can be a name of a person, place, or thing. The name should be considered as a noun. Recall our prior discussion on 'Noun Search and Analysis'.

Under these circumstances, a taxonomy will not work at all for name recognition. The best bet for capturing names is using inline contextualization.

Snippets

When doing analysis on text, it is almost always helpful to have as much context as is possible. It is one thing to look at a list of Marys:

- Mary at page 35
- Mary at page 120
- Mary at page 625

When you look at the raw list of Marys and the address or the location, the name tells you very little other than the fact that someone named Mary exists at a certain location.

It often helps a lot if the analyzed word is in the form of a snippet. A snippet is the text immediately preceding and following the word. In the form of a snippet the following list of Marys has a whole different connotation:

- Mary had a little lamb at page 35
- Mary Levins wrote a book at page 120
- Bloody Mary's at 5:00 pm on the deck at page 625

When words are in a snippet format, it is much more enlightening to make sense of the word's meaning. Snippets can provide valuable context.

Linking Text

Another useful feature is the linking of text. On occasion, one portion of text references another portion of text. There are many ways to link text.

"…liquor license…."

"…liquor license (AZ12-87729)…."

"… liquor license (Doc FGH)…"

Fig 8.9 Linking related text.

Simple Disambiguation

Disambiguation refers to the removal of ambiguity by making something clear. Disambiguation narrows down the meaning of words, and it's a good thing. This word makes sense if you break it down. Dis means "not," ambiguous means "unclear," and the ending -tion makes it a noun.

Textual disambiguation is an iterative process.

One of the challenges the analyst faces is that of disambiguating text. As a simple example of disambiguation of text, suppose we had the sentence:

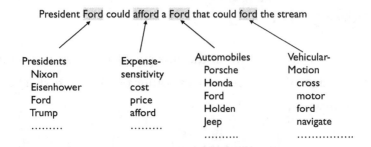

Fig 8.10 A simple example of disambiguation.

President Ford could be recognized because the name is in Caps, and it is preceded by President. Ford is part of the word – afford. Ford standing alone and in caps refers to an automobile. And ford standing alone in an uncapitalized form represents a form of vehicular motion.

To execute textual disambiguation, it is necessary to "map" a document to the appropriate parameters that can be specified inside textual disambiguation. The mapping directs textual disambiguation as to how the document needs to be interpreted. The mapping process is similar to the process of designing how a system will operate. Each document has its own mapping process.

The mapping parameters are specified and on completion of the mapping process, a document can then be executed. The same mapping can serve all documents of the same type. For example, there may be one mapping for contracts, another mapping for resume management, another mapping for call analysis, and so on.

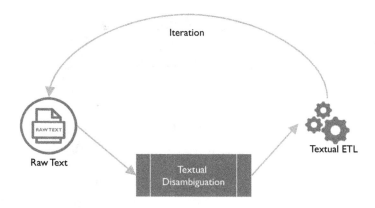

Fig 8.11 The iterative process.

So textual disambiguation is an iterative process. Once the mapping is created, you process a few documents through it, then the analyst needs to check and validate the result. After the review, the analyst may decide to do some necessary changes to the mapping specification(s). Then again, the document is processed through the new mapping specs. This process keeps going iteratively till the analyst is not satisfied with the ultimate output/result of the textual disambiguation.

Textual disambiguation is sometimes called textual ETL. Textual disambiguation consists of many different algorithms. The two most prominent algorithms are document fracturing and inline contextualization (sometimes called "value process"). The mapping process precedes identifying documents that need to be processed through textual disambiguation. The iterative approach is the way that documents are normally processed.

Same Word/Multiple Taxonomies

In the same vein, it is certainly possible for the same word to appear in different taxonomies.

The more he drank, the more he began to slur his speech…

The guitar piece required a slur before the final notes…

The politicians words were a slur against the nation….

Music	Negativity	Speech
bar	barb	pronunciation
clef	derogatory	accent
note	slur	slur
slur	cheap shot	diction
stop	………………	………………
….		

Fig 8.12 The same word can appear in multiple taxonomies.

Words and Strings

There is a difference between searching for a word and searching for a string. Under normal circumstances, the search is done for a string. Suppose you had the string = "search" – entered into your system. The system would find all occurrences of the string "search." It would find "search," "searched," "searching," "searches," etc.

Search
Searching
Searched   Look for "search"
Searches
Searcher

Fig 8.13 The results of looking for a string.

Now suppose you wanted to find only the word "search." If you enter the word you are looking for in brackets – [search] - the system knows to find only the single word "search." If you used brackets around "search" you would not find "searched," "searching," "searches," etc. However, this might be a tool-specific feature/search criterion, and the annotation can be different for other same purpose tool(s). In the same vein, you can specify phrases that consist of more than one word as search criteria.

"hot dog"
"King Henry"
"President Ford"

Fig 8.14 The usage of multiple words.

CHAPTER 9

Architecture

While the textual warehouse is a good way to manage data in the corporation, there are long-term and strategic implications. A good place to start our architectural exploration is examining a more familiar architecture – the data warehouse environment.

The Data Warehouse Environment

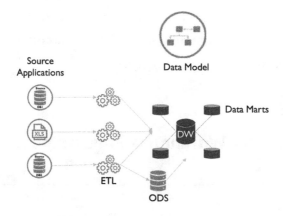

Fig 9.1 The classical data warehouse architecture.

Classically the components of the data warehouse environment are:

- Applications – typically transaction processing applications

- ETL transformation processing – where application data is transformed into corporate data

- The ODS (operational data store) – where integrated transaction processing occurs

- The data model – where data is abstracted

- The data warehouse – the integrated, historical foundation of reliable data

- Data marts that reflect the views of different departments, such as marketing, sales, finance, etc.

The classical data warehouse environment is explained at length in other books and articles. Our interest in the data warehouse environment is in how it compares to the textual warehouse environment.

The Textual Warehouse Environment

Textual ETL is designed for reading and processing text. Classical ETL is designed for handling data from a database. But the data found in either warehouse (Textual warehouse or Data Warehouse) is able to be immediately and easily traced back to its source.

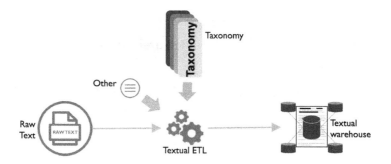

Fig 9.2 The textual warehouse environment.

The components of the textual warehouse are:

- Raw text – text from many different types of sources
- Taxonomies – classifications of text
- Textual ETL – code that reads text and turns text into a database
- Textual warehouse – the integrated store of textual information

Raw text in the textual warehouse is the equivalent of applications in the data warehouse. Of course, raw text can be from any source.

The taxonomies that are found in the textual warehouse are exactly the same kind of taxonomies that are found in the data warehouse.

Textual ETL is significantly different from classical ETL. Textual ETL is designed for reading and processing text. Classical ETL is designed for handling data from a database. The data warehouse is designed to hold transactional data. The textual warehouse is designed to handle text of any variety. In both cases, the data found in either warehouse can be immediately and easily traced back to its source.

Linkage

When the data warehouse environment and the textual warehouse environment are in the same environment or are closely related, it is possible to link the data from the two environments. The linkage of the two environments can analytically produce different and elegant results.

While it is possible to link the two environments, the linkage is still an indirect one. For example, the database in the data warehouse environment will have keys. The keys from the data warehouse will have little or no linkage to the textual warehouse. However, other data in the data warehouse record may well have data that forms a linkage. For example, the data warehouse may have the state of Texas and golf clubs that are mentioned in the data warehouse environment. The textual warehouse may have a taxonomy for states that includes Texas. In addition, there may be a taxonomy that includes golf clubs. By using these two classifications of text, a linkage can be formed between a text warehouse and a data warehouse.

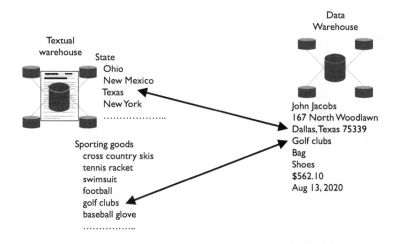

Fig 9.3 Indirect linkage between the two environments.

There may be other types of linkages between the two environments. There may be a linkage between the taxonomy and the data model.

Linking Taxonomies and Data Models

Fig 9.4 Comparing taxonomies to data models.

There are, however, differences between the data model and the taxonomy. The taxonomy contains specific words or phrases, such as Porsche, Ford, and Honda, while the data model does not contain specific references to objects. The data model contains generic references to objects (as opposed to specific references).

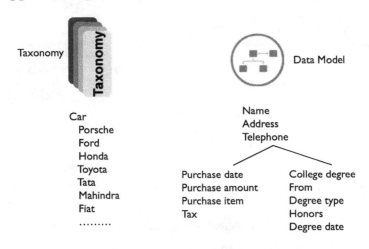

Fig 9.5 Differences in the kinds of data.

The Flow of Information

There is a flow of information from the raw text to the analytical stage in the textual warehouse. Data starts at the raw text level. Data flows through the textual ETL environment where it is vetted by a taxonomy. The data then flows into the textual warehouse. Once in the textual warehouse, the text can be analyzed by the textual analytics workbench. Analysis can be done there or inside a spreadsheet. Once the analysis is done, the analyst can return to the starting point with a new set of requirements.

New input can take many forms. It can be a change to the taxonomy. It can be a change to the input. It can be specialized editing of the input. In short, when analysis is done, iterative changes to that analysis can entail practically anything.

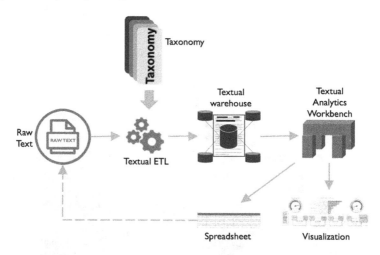

Fig 9.6 The changes that can be made as part of iterative processing.

Probability of Access

When you look at the textual warehouse environment and the data warehouse environment, one way of comparing the content is through the probability of access. Some parts of the environment have a very predictable and constant stream of access. Other parts of the environment have a low or sporadic rate of access.

Different Usages

Along with the different access rates, there are different types of usage of data found throughout the different environments.

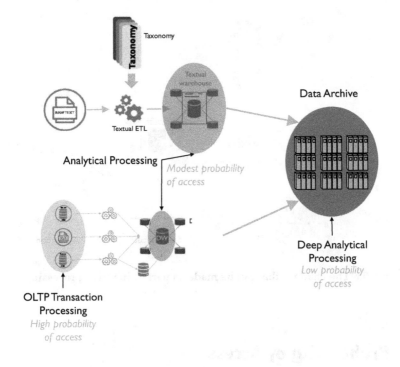

Fig 9.7 The different kinds of processing that can occur.

There is online, high-performance transaction processing that occurs in the OLTP transaction environment. Analytical processing occurs in the warehouse. And historical analytic processing occurs in the archival environment.

CHAPTER 10

Medical Records Example

Once upon a time, about 2000 years ago, a young Greek girl was walking down a path carrying an urn. History does not tell us why she did this, but this young lady put the urn down on the ground and never returned. Maybe she went swimming in the ocean. Maybe at that very moment, the Spartans launched an attack and she had to flee for her life. We don't know why she never returned to retrieve her urn on the ground.

After a year there was some dust on the urn. After ten years the urn was covered with dust. After a hundred years the urn was covered with dirt. After a millennium, the urn was buried under the earth. After two millennium the urn was six feet under the earth.

As every year passed, slowly the urn gathered more and more dirt and dust until the point arrived where it was buried underneath the earth. And with each new layer of dust and dirt, the urn became increasingly more difficult to find and retrieve. The process of burying the urn was slow and gradual but inevitable. Finally, archaeologists discovered the urn. But it took a huge effort to locate and retrieve the urn. Time has a way of burying things. The burial occurs in an evolutionary manner.

Time and Text

For any kind of text, once time buries text, the text becomes harder and harder to find and retrieve.

Time buries text just as it buries the Grecian urn. And once time buries text, the text becomes harder and harder to find and retrieve. This is true for all kinds of text – contracts, medical records, memos, and email. All text is subject to the ravages of time.

A Medical Record

To start our story of the evolution that occurs over time, suppose we start with a medical record. A medical record is created when a patient has an encounter with a healthcare provider. The patient may have a procedure done. The patient may have a cold. The patient may have a case of COVID. There is almost an infinite number of reasons why the doctor creates a medical record. In any case, a record is created that memorializes the results of the medical encounter.

```
Medical developments Night
- D36 ICU
- Neurological deficit (PC)
- Epilepsy
- Pneumonia + V. Mechanics
- Prolonged IRPA
Patient with clinical steady, afebrile, acianóticom well adapted to mechanical ventilation in spontaneously - PSV:. PEEP 14: 5 OT: 370
ml Fr: 21 FiO2: 0.25 Patient was shaky, but the situation was dealt with placement blanket on the patient (cold). Tax: 36.4 C
LCA: RCR HR: 79 bpm PA: 158x107 mm Hg
Remaining unchanged physical examination.
Diuresis: 1600 ml 8H/12h: - 550 ml
Conduct: Support unchanged
SERGIO RICARDO LOBO LOUREIRO Medico
02/06/2009
17:58
PHYSIOTHERAPY
Patient awake, follows in VM / PSV, PS 18, PEEP: 5, FIO2 25%, keeping VC and SpO2 satisfactory. PS I reduce. Follow so far no signs of
respiratory effort. Secretive, cough present the stimulus, with a moderate amount of mucopurulent secretion in TQT + drooling.
AR: MV + without RA.
CD: Respiratory physiotherapy and motor. Aspirations of TQT and VAS. Adjustments in the VM. Functional positioning in bed.
ADRIANA SILVA MARIZ physiotherapist
02/06/2009
17:37
Patient follow agreed on mechanical ventilation with FiO2 25% and 95% saturation. Normotensive, afebril.Apresenta quite tracheal
secretions and especially sialorreia.Dieta by SNE with good aceitação.Diurese good spontaneous gift debit.
Geraldo Silva Celso Machado nurse
02/06/2009
14:03
ICU-HRSAM
```

Fig 10.1 A simple doctor/patient medical record.

Medical records are important to the health of a patient. The medications taken at age 60 and the procedures done at age 50 may have a direct relationship to the medications and treatments of the patient at age 30. A patient's medical history plays a vital role in determining the day-to-day treatment prescribed by the doctor. And medical records are not only important to the individual patient, but medical records are also important collectively, across multiple patients and across vistas of time.

A Cabinet

After the doctor/patient record is created, what happens to it? If the medical practice is young and new and there aren't many other patients or medical records in the practice, the record may be put into a simple filing cabinet.

As long as there aren't too many other records in the cabinet, the medical record is safe, secure, and easy to find.

For the longest time, there is no problem in the storing of medical records in a cabinet. But soon, other doctors join the practice, and they start creating their own records. The problem is that the records created by the new doctors are in different formats. Each doctor has his/her own way of creating a medical record. This inconsistency of format makes searching for and finding medical records difficult.

A Standardized Medical Record

One day the doctors decide to create their own standardized medical record.

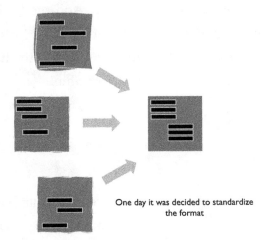

One day it was decided to standardize
the format

Fig 10.2 The move to standardize the way that medical records are created by each of the doctors.

After the record format is standardized, the small number of older records is converted to the new format. And all new records added to the file are in the new format. Once the conversion is made, it is much easier to find medical records in the filing cabinet.

Then there are more records and more cabinets

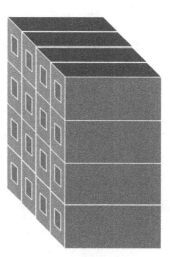

Fig 10.3 As time passes, there are more and more records and more cabinets that are needed to hold the records.

There starts to be a problem with the filing cabinet holding all of the medical records. If a file is removed and then placed back into the cabinet, and if the file is placed in the wrong place, the file may never be found again. To search for a misplaced file, the analyst has to search sequentially through the entire cabinet manually. Such a task is burdensome and is truly unwelcome. Yet, that is what it takes to find a misplaced file in the face of a large filing cabinet of records.

Time continues to pass and the need for even more cabinet space continues to grow. The paper grows thin and weak. The paper becomes dogeared. If left in the sun, the ink starts to fade. Over time the paper starts to deteriorate.

Enter the Electronic Medical Record

Finally, one day the number of records simply overwhelms the healthcare provider. Physically storing the records in a cabinet is no longer an option. The organization decides to go to an electronic medical record (an EHR). So, the organization chooses some EHR (electronic hospital record) technology. A standard package for creating an electronic version of the cabinets was created.

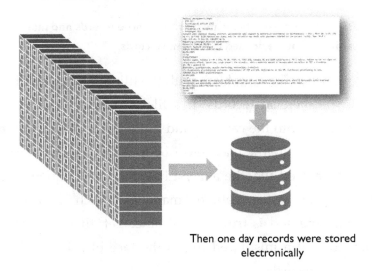

Then one day records were stored
electronically

Fig 10.4 The expanded cabinets that were created.

The function of the cabinets remains the same. It is just that now the cabinets are store electronically, inside a database.

One of the issues facing the organization is what to do about all of the older records stored on paper? It is found that most of the data found in the very earliest of records is seldom accessed. So the decision is made to convert only the newest paper records. Some of the records remain in a paper format in the cabinet. Some of the records are converted to an electronic format.

Once the records could be added and managed electronically, it becomes much easier to add records to the collection. Soon there was a flood of new records. The new records greatly expanded the databases. Everything worked fine. Records were added, and the databases grew.

Changing Vendors

Then one day, the organization decided to switch vendors for the creation and storage of electronic medical records. There could be multiple reasons for this switch:

- New functionality needed
- A streamlined and eloquent sales effort
- Industry pressure

And very shortly, different kinds of medical records were being stored. Some of the records were converted from the old system to the new system. But many records were not converted. This caused some difficulty because now in order to find anything, the doctor had to search two different kinds of electronic records.

Other Types of Records

Adding to the confusion was the fact that, mixed with the medical records, there were other types of records that were being stored electronically along with the medical records, including:

- Insurance records
- Payment and billing records
- Legal tort records
- Medical research records

At this point, it became difficult to find anything. There were lots of reasons why finding anything was difficult:

- The sheer number of records
- The different formats of records
- The fact that many records were spread over multiple systems and multiple media
- The diverse mixture of records

In addition, those records still on a non-electronic media continue to deteriorate.

Doing Medical Research

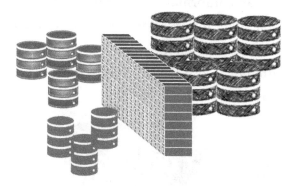

Soon records were everywhere
- different formats
- different media
- different technologies

Fig 10.5 The dilemma facing anyone wanting to do medical research in a hospital.

The reaction of the analyst trying to do research was, "why can't I find anything?" "Why are there all of these obstacles waiting for me that defeat my efforts to try to efficiently and accurately find information?"

Frustration In Doing Research

It is one thing to try to find information on a single patient. It is another thing altogether to try to research a multitude of records. Many problems await the analyst that wants to look across multiple record types:

- Records are scattered
- The same information appears in different names
- Some older information has deteriorated to the point of inaccessibility
- Different record formats hold the same information

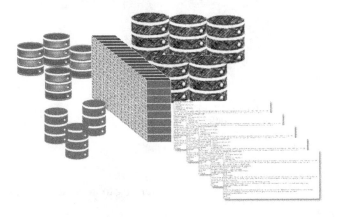

Fig 10.6 Trying to do research on multiple records is impossible.

This scenario is for medical records in a hospital. But the same scenario is true for many different environments, other than the healthcare environment, including:

- Insurance companies
- Banks
- Finance organizations
- Airlines
- Restaurant chains
- Engineering/manufacturing organizations
- And many more

The Problem and its classification

So, based on our discussion so far under this case study, irrespective of the domain/industry/business, if we look into the core business problem(s), they can be classified as follows:

- Valuable non-electronic records/ old records
- Non-standard format/data captured
- Rapidly growing volume of data

In terms of medical records, challenges include medical research hurdles, patient diagnosis challenges as the history of medical records were not arranged and retrieved on time, and various analytical challenges while using the medical records of that short.

The Solution

There can be multiple solutions to address the above-listed problem classifications. We have discussed it in this chapter and how few problems were addressed on an adhoc basis wherever and whenever it was incountered. But those were proved not to be a sustainable solution.

Few other possible solutions can be medical transcription and digitization of medical records from scratch. But medical transcription is an expensive solution in this era where we can opt for highly economical and feasible solutions using textual ETL and a textual warehouse.

The textual warehouse can address the underlying problems discussed in this case study, where textual ETL will help bring all such uncaptured medical records to a structured database form for better analysis and search. To help the medical research work and to connect dots between all historical patient records for better diagnosis. It can help the analyst develop correlative analysis and help other medical feternity benefit from the abundant potential medical records in possession.

Healthcare and medical science has more than 600 thousands medical terminologies that cover diversified and vast medical domain. It is one of the largest domain-based terminology groups in the world. A rich taxonomy of medical records used in the textual ETL to bring the text to the textual warehouse will help map almost all possible medical records and bring life to those so-called abandoned medical records for the benefit of the healthcare industry and the profession, with its textual analytics support capabilities along with its unique power of contextualization and correlation enablement. Textual Warehouse is economical, seamless, scalable, sustainable, and future proof solution to any such problem.

Textual warehouse usage for COVID treatment

In this use case, we will see how the textual warehouse is extremely useful with medical records. Suppose the analyst wants to find patients who have had COVID. Once those patients are located, the analysis then centers on two things: How has COVID affected the patient? What prior medications has the patient taken prior to contracting COVID? Is there a relationship between the medications taken before having COVID that have affected the severity of the reaction to COVID?

To answer this question, it is necessary to look into the text found in many records of patients.

To answer this question, the analyst needs to look deeply into the patients' medical records who have contracted COVID. The data that is needed to answer this question is in the textual warehouse.

First, the analyst looks for patients who have had COVID. Then the analyst classifies the patients into several categories: patients who have had a severe reaction to COVID (or who have died). Then there are patients who had COVID who had a reaction, but not a severe reaction. Then there are patients who had COVID and hardly knew they had it. After the identification and the classification has been done, the analyst then looks back into the medical records for each patient identifying what medications they have taken throughout their life. Then the results are correlated.

The textual warehouse can be helpful for analysis of any specific type of cardiovascular disease, various endocrinology complexities, and specific oncology case analysis.

CHAPTER 11

Industry Examples

The advantages of the textual warehouse are many and obvious. The textual warehouse saves space, allows text to be found at its most detailed level, sets the stage for archival processing, and generally complements the overall data architecture of the organization. The textual warehouse is an architectural asset.

But how does the textual warehouse enhance the day-to-day business of the organization? There is no better explanation than to look at some good examples.

How many policies have expanded coverage?

A question an insurance executive may be interested in is, How many policies have expanded coverage? And what kind of coverages are there?

To answer this question thoroughly and accurately, it is necessary to go back through every policy and identify and quantify what is meant by expanded coverage. Does expanded coverage mean liability? Does expanded coverage cover automobiles? Cars? Motorcycles? Does expanded coverage encompass corporate liability as well as personal liability? What about home insurance? To find out what is meant by expanded coverage, it is necessary to go into the actual text that encompasses the coverage that is of interest.

With the textual warehouse, this analysis is performed electronically instead of being done manually.

In addition, there is the element of time. Is the query looking at all current policies in force? Is the time frame go back to 1970? What changes have occurred since 1970? What laws have changed? Going backward in time is a challenge because business practices change, laws change, economic conditions change, and so forth.

To answer this question thoroughly and accurately, it is necessary to go back and look at the textual specifics of each policy.

What is the total exposure to the forthcoming hurricane?

In the same vein, consider the question the insurance executive may be interested in – what is the total exposure to the hurricane just off the Florida coast that will be coming inland in the next few days?

To answer this question, the analyst needs to know some things about the hurricane. What is the projected path of the hurricane? Will it go inland to South Carolina? Will it head out to sea? What is the strength of the hurricane? How much is the sea level supposed to rise during storm surge? Where will storm surge be the greatest?

Once the analyst knows what these projections are, the analyst can start to make projections about how bad the storm will be and what path it will take. Armed with that information, the analyst can identify which policies and which policyholders will be affected. Once the policyholders are identified, the coverages of each policyholder can be calculated. In addition, an estimation of the damage can be projected.

In addition to helping the analyst, this work will help the actuary and the actuary process to determine insurance premium calculations. In fact, the textual warehouse can help a lot and contribute tremendously to the actuary process. It will help make accurate risk and premium calculations. It can arm the actuary with ample information required to bring accuracy to the actuary calculations.

What about COVID-related insurance coverage?

The textual warehouse is useful well beyond the healthcare and medical records. The textual warehouse is also useful in the estimation of coverage. Suppose the analyst wants to find patients who have had COVID and with health insurance. Once those patients are located, we can determine which states, cities, zones, and areas are most impacted, the segment of patients and their level of severity, the claim percentage with respect to other claims, the period of the claim, the duration of hospitalization, and the claim's impact on the overall health insurance business. It will help the actuaries calculate the premium for the covid coverage.

Answering this question requires the analyst to look deeply into health insurance claims and medical records (exposed in line with the applicable healthcare data protection policies) of the patients who have contracted COVID. In this case, medical records might not always be mandatory but instead optional, as the required information is submitted by the providers to the payers while submitting the claims. The data that is needed to answer these questions appears in the textual warehouse.

First, the analyst looks for patients who have had COVID. Then the analyst classifies the patients into several categories including patients who died due to COVID.

Resolving Historical Claims

Looking across vast vistas of information can be done with the textual warehouse. But there are other uses as well.

Suppose the analyst wishes to settle an estate of someone who has just passed away. Part of the estate settlement requires that the analyst go back and see exactly what the terms of the account were at the time of the purchase (of the life insurance policy, the annuity, or whatever instrument the deceased owned). The problem is that the account was purchased in 1935. In 1935 the records were all kept manually. Trying to go back and reconstruct the old information is a challenge. It must be done, and it must be done quickly, fairly, and honestly.

With a textual warehouse, it is easy enough to go back and find the particulars of a document from 1935. The textual warehouse will have the information as to exactly where the document is and what it says. Being able to find older documents is one of the major values of a textual warehouse.

You can refer to the exact document and all the identifying, qualifying, and simple text of the document. You will have the data even ready for analysis whenever and wherever needed.

A Conduit to Other Records

There are other uses of the textual warehouse. One use of the textual warehouse is as a conduit to other records. In other words, the textual warehouse can be used to connect with different types of records.

Consider the question, *For patients who have had treatment XYZ, what have the outcomes been?* In this case, it is not enough to find one type of record and then perform analysis. It is necessary to locate one kind of record and then locate another type of related record. The first step is to find patients treated with XYZ. The next step is to find later records which describe the outcome of the treatment.

Here it might not be important that which patient's treatment for XYZ is what. But think about the broader picture. What is important is to find out what exactly happened to the XYZ treatment altogether. And the information extracted with the help of the textual warehouse can be so important that it can be used as a learning for doctors, hospitals, and healthcare professionals to treat other patients with similar complications. Here the textual warehouse helped you know in advance or helped you learn what will be the exact treatment of XYZ and the outcome.

The textual warehouse is useful for finding the different types of records needed for the analysis.

In a Corporate Merger and Acquisition

Another place where the textual warehouse is needed is in doing a corporate merger or acquisition. The considerations of mergers and acquisitions are many and complex. The textual warehouse holds the key to understanding the issues of a merger or acquisition. Once the textual warehouse is built, the analyst is just a query away from finding out all sorts of information:

- Terms there are in the contracts
- Deadlines
- Penalties
- Sales commitments

This information and more is important to the merger and acquisition of a company. To find out these kinds of information quickly and accurately is a great advantage in the negotiation process of a merger and acquisition.

The Anatomy of an Analysis

When you step back and look at the query and analysis process, it is obvious the role that the textual warehouse plays. The textual warehouse can be positioned with other parts of the infrastructure.

> *The textual warehouse sits between the data warehouse and the archives of the corporation.*

Some corporations have well-organized, easy-to-access archives and other companies have messy, poorly organized archives. And some corporations have archives not organized at all. But even for the tiniest, most poorly organized companies, somewhere there is an archive.

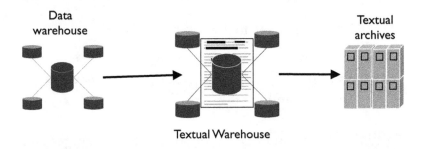

Fig 11.1 Where the textual warehouse is positioned.

When it is time to do analysis, if the analysis is of the operational variety involving transactional processing, the logical place to look is the data warehouse. Given that the data warehouse is all electronic and well organized (if it has been built properly), the data warehouse is easy and fast to query.

Now suppose the query and analysis process needs to include text. The textual warehouse sits ready and available to provide its information. And if there is a further need to go into the archives of the organization, at the very least, the textual warehouse provides a guideline to as to where to look.

The data warehouse and the textual warehouse provide a foundation for joint queries that involve both transactional information and textual information of the business.

In addition, taken together, the data warehouse and the textual warehouse provide a foundation for joint queries that involve both transactional information and textual information.

CHAPTER 12

Textual Warehouse Evolution

The textual warehouse is just another step in the evolution of architecture. Like all evolutions, the textual warehouse takes a long time to become apparent as an architectural feature of technology. Evolutions move with the speed of a glacier. To architecturally appreciate the evolution of the textual warehouse, it is necessary to step back and look at the evolution of computer architecture.

Simple Systems

In the earliest days – in the dawn of the computer profession, there were simple systems. These systems essentially started to do in an automated manner what was once done manually. These early systems were simple and limited in scope. They mimicked what was done manually. The business value of these early systems was the substitution of the computer for a human.

If you taught them well, computers could do rote work cheaper, faster, and more accurately than human beings.

Typical of simple systems were accounts payable, accounts receivable, paycheck printing, and human resources. For the most part, the business value accomplished by these systems was significant but tangential to the mainline of the business.

The technology used in these early systems was punch cards, paper tape, magnetic tape files, and printed reports.

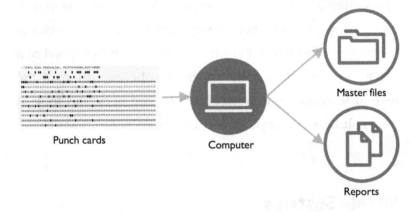

Punch cards   Computer   Master files

Reports

Fig 12.1 The earliest automation.

Online Transaction Processing

For various reasons, the first-generation computer systems were replaced by a much more powerful, much more sophisticated type of technology. That technology was disk-based and included a database management system. Soon the world had online transaction processing (OLTP) systems. And with OLTP systems came a breakthrough in business value. For the first time, the computer entered into the mainstream world of business. Because data could be accessed quickly and directly, it was possible to do online processing.

Suddenly the computer became essential to the mainline, day to day business of the corporation. Soon there were reservation systems, bank teller processing systems, ATM systems, and so forth. Soon business could not operate without their computer. When the computer system went down, the business suffered.

The technology typical of this generation of technology were disk storage, database management systems, cathode ray tubes, reports, and large-scale transaction processing computers.

The data in this environment was very current– an hour old, a day old, or even a week old. But any amount of other historical data was scrapped in keeping the system free of unnecessary data to improve performance.

The business value of this generation of technology was immediate and obvious. Computers ran the day-to-day business of the organization. Without the computer, the business would not operate efficiently or at all.

After textual ETL is available, text could be incorporated into the mainstream business decision making.

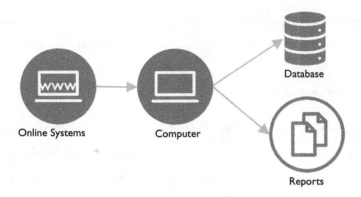

Fig 12.2 The second generation of computerized technology (OLTP).

Integrity of Data

The second generation of computerized architecture was so successful that soon systems were popping up everywhere. Soon there were computer systems of every variety doing all sorts of tasks. And with this proliferation of computers and systems came an endemic problem – the integrity of data. There was no shortage of data in this environment. The problem was that there was so much data that people did not know what to believe. The same data element had one value in one place and ten other values in ten other places. You could lay your hands-on data, but you had no idea if the data was correct.

Next came the data warehouse. The data warehouse became the "system of record" for information. In some circles, the data warehouse was the "single version of the truth." If an organization were looking for accurate information, they looked to the data warehouse.

Along with the data warehouse came the opportunity to do analytical processing. Analytical processing allowed the business to think ahead and start to see the larger picture emerging in the corporation's world. Previously the computer had been used for day-to-day decisions. Now the computer could be used for analytical decisions.

The business value of being able to do analytical processing cannot be quantified. Every business has the need to be able to do analytical processing.

One other feature of the data warehouse was that, for the first time, historical data was recognized and accommodated. Before the data warehouse, there was little or no accommodation for historical data. The OLTP environment looked at very immediate data as did the first generation of computer technology. But with the data warehouse, the vista of data over five to ten years worth of time was accommodated.

There is the argument that only very current data is worthwhile. And in a way that is a valid viewpoint. But when you consider that customers are creatures of habit, knowing the patterns of buying established early on in life leads to an understanding of those patterns at a later point in life. There is then powerful justification in storing and examining historical data.

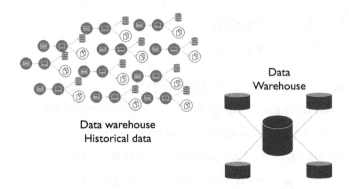

Data warehouse
Historical data

Data
Warehouse

Fig 12.3 The advent of the data warehouse.

After the data warehouse had become established, it became apparent that a huge amount of data in the corporation was not being made available to the corporation. That data was textual data. For a variety of reasons, text did not fit well with standard database technology. Text never was treated prominently. But when textual ETL became available suddenly, text could be incorporated into the mainstream decision-making of the corporation.

To organize and accommodate all of the text in the corporation, it was necessary to build a textual warehouse. In many ways, the textual warehouse was the companion of the data warehouse. The textual warehouse made available the textual information in the corporation that once had been off-limits. Suddenly two new types of processing became available:

- Text only analysis
- Mixed text and data analysis

The ability to process text opened up the doors to many types of applications in the corporation. Contracts analysis, call center analysis, Internet sentiment analysis, medical records analysis, product quality report analysis, process log analysis, and many other types of analysis became possible. After the textual warehouse came the formalization of archival systems. There were three business values to archival systems:

- The possibility of doing analysis inside the archival system.
- The removal of older archival data to "get out of the way" of fresher data.
- The need to satisfy litigated requirements for the storage of records.

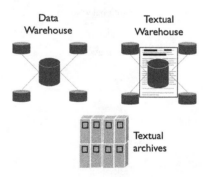

Fig 12.4 The advent of archival systems.

The evolution of computer architecture occurs at a rapid pace compared to other evolutions. The evolution of computer architecture occurs in response to fulfilling some business need.

The Stages of the Evolution

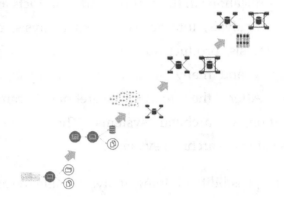

Fig 12.5 The evolution of architecture.

Linearly, the different stages of the evolution have passed through the following passages.

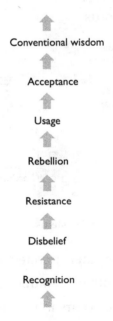

Conventional wisdom

Acceptance

Usage

Rebellion

Resistance

Disbelief

Recognition

Fig 12.6 The phases of architectural evolution.

The first phase is recognition of the need for change. The people that do this kind of work are visionaries. Next comes disbelief. Nobody believes the visionaries. Then comes resistance. People try to block change. Next comes rebellion. People openly rebel against the idea of change. Next comes usage. Usage normally occurs when the obstacle to change is removed. Usage normally occurs in groups outside of the technical community. After enough usage occurs, next comes acceptance by the marketplace. And after acceptance comes conventional wisdom.

As we learned so far, to address the problem of finding the textual data in your corporation, you need a textual warehouse. A textual warehouse is similar to a data warehouse except that it applies only to text and to documents.

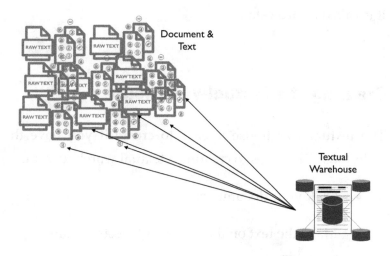

Fig 12.7 The textual warehouse helps find organizational text- and document-based data

In other words, we can say that the textual warehouse is similar to a data warehouse except that it exists solely for the purpose of enabling the organization to find its text/document based data. In many ways, the textual warehouse serves the same function as a card catalog in a library. In a large library, there is a wide collection of knowledge and books. You would never want to walk into a library and look for a book by walking up and down the stacks of books and examining each book. If you tried such an approach, you would be in the library for months at a time. Instead, you go into the library and use the card catalog to direct you to where you want to go. In doing so, you save endless amounts of time uselessly doing a search.

Libraries have known about and have used a textual warehouse for a long time now. As mentioned, in a library it is called a card catalog.

Creating the Textual Warehouse

The textual warehouse is easy to create if you have the right tools. The steps to creating a textual warehouse are:

- OCR your documents

- Make the text on the document electronically readable

- Pass your text through textual ETL using an appropriate taxonomy or taxonomies

- Create a small "working" textual warehouse

- Load your working textual warehouse into your larger corporate textual warehouse

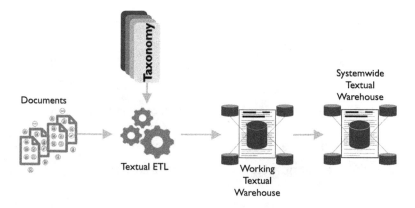

Fig 12.8 System-wide textual warehouse.

As a rule, you create your system-wide textual warehouse incrementally, one project at a time. You can start to use your system-wide textual warehouse as soon as you start to add data. But the system-wide textual warehouse is not complete until all documents have been processed. And of course, as new documents enter the system, they are processed and are placed into the textual warehouse.

In many ways, the textual warehouse is the analogical equivalent to the operational data repository.

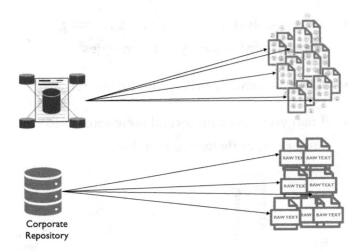

Fig 12.9 System-wide textual warehouse vs. corporate repository.

There really are two types of content to the textual warehouse: mandated data and optional data.

Mandated Data

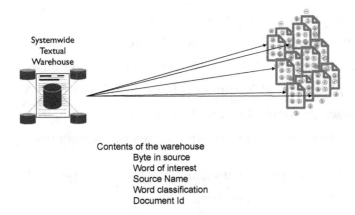

Fig 12.10 The mandated data in the textual warehouse.

One type of mandated data is the source name. The source name is the name the system knows the document by. Another type of mandated data is the byte address of the word referenced in the document. Another mandated type of data is the document id. This is the external name the document is known by, outside of the computer system. Next there is the word of interest, which is the referenced word. Then there is the word classification, which is the taxonomical reference to the word of interest.

These then are the required types of data of every document in the textual warehouse.

Optional Data

But you can include other types of data in the textual warehouse.

Some of the other types of data that in the textual warehouse include:

- The date of creation of the document
- The language the document is in
- The author of the document
- The place the document was created
- The length of the document, etc.

In fact, you can include any kind of data that you wish in the textual warehouse.

Once you have built the textual warehouse, you can have immediate end-user access to the documents within your organization.

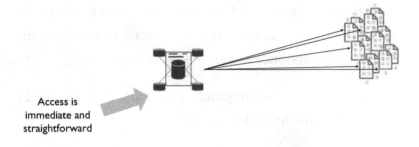

Access is immediate and straightforward

Fig 12.10 Immediate access.

Now you can find documents and text easily throughout your company easily and quickly.

Reinforce Your Reading

1. Most business decisions are based upon what percentage of enterprise data?

(a). 10%.

(b). 50%.

(c). 75%.

(d). 90%.

2. Which leads to high quality OCR results?

(a). Use of supported fonts.

(b). Paper quality is good.

(c). Print quality is good.

(d). All of the above.

3. When should we transcribe documents?

(a). When most of the documents were not processed well through OCR.

(b). When manual processing is not possible due to the size and volume of documents.

(c). For handwritten documents or voice files.

(d). All the above.

4. How do you save space when processing boilerplate documents?

(a). You save as '.txt'.

(b). You save as '.xml'.

(c). You save the results once and then reference it.

(d). You reduce the font size.

5. Which are not contents of the Textual Warehouse?

(a). Unique identifier of a record.

(b). Byte address of the word in the document.

(c). Foreign keys.

(d). Classification of the word.

(e). Source file location.

6. Ontology is group of _____ taxonomies.

(a). easy

(b). complex

(c). related

(d). asymmetric

7. Taxonomies can come from:

(a). Commercial vendor.

(b). Raw text.

(c). Thesaurus.

(d). All the above.

8. A Taxonomy is to Text what a Data Model is to a _____:

(a). Database.

(b). Raw Text.

(c). Data.

(d). Normalization.

9. To create a textual warehouse, raw text passes through:

(a). A database.

(b). A file system.

(c). Textual ETL.

(d). Standard ETL.

10. True or False, textual ETL output storage is database agnostic?

11. Source of a textual warehouse can be:
(a). .txt
(b). .docx
(c). .pdf
(d). Any or all of the above.

12. Textual ETL does:
(a). Taxonomic resolution.
(b). Stop word resolution.
(c). Alternate spelling resolution.
(d). Homographic resolution.
(e). All of the above.

13. If a classic data warehouse has a data model, a textual warehouse has a:
(a). graph.
(b). node.
(c). taxonomy.
(d). blueprint.

14. True or False, classic data warehouse requirements are mostly changing, but textual warehouse requirements are always static?

15. True or False, in Textual ETL, 'taxonomies' are used when text is unpredictable?

16. True or False, in Textual ETL, 'inline contextualization' is used when text is unpredictable?

17. True or False, textual disambiguation is an iterative process?

18. True or False, data found in a textual warehouse is easily and quickly traced back to its source?

19. Why is a textual warehouse required for an insurance company?

(a). Insurance has contracts containing a lot of text.

(b). For faster resolution of historical claims, old contracts need to be retrieved faster.

(c). Historic data in insurance contracts offers insight to the present business.

(d). All of above.

20. Which is the right sequence to create a textual warehouse?

I. Make the text on the document electronically readable.

II. Pass your text through textual ETL using appropriate taxonomies.

III. Create a large corporate textual warehouse.

IV. Create an org wise small working textual warehouse.

(a). I-II-III-IV

(b). II-I-III-IV

(c). I-II-IV-III

(d). VI-II-III-I

Answers:

1. a
2. d
3. d
4. c
5. c
6. c
7. d
8. a
9. c
10. True
11. d
12. e
13. c
14. False
15. True
16. False
17. True
18. True
19. d
20. c

Index

www.ingramcontent.com/pod-product-compliance
Lightning Source LLC
Chambersburg PA
CBHW071249050326
40690CB00011B/2323